STUFFED SPUDS

STUFFED SPUDS

100 Light Meals in a Potato

JEANNE JONES

CASTLE BOOKS

Published in 1994 by
CASTLE BOOKS
A division of Book Sales, Inc.
P.O. Box 7100
Edison, NJ 08818-7100

Published by arrangement with M. Evans and Company, Inc.,
216 East 49th Street, New York, NY 10017.

ISBN 0-7858-0281-9

Library of Congress Cataloging-in-Publication Data

Jones, Jeanne.
    Stuffed spuds: 100 light meals in a potato / Jeanne Jones.
    p.
    Includes index.

    1. Cookery (Potatoes)   2. Cookery (Entrées)
I. Title.
TX803-P8J66   1992
641.6'521 – dc20   92-6868

Design by RFS Graphic Design, Inc.

Printed in the U.S.A.

TO DICK DUFFY

My favorite Irishman, whose ancestors made this book possible by bringing potatoes to this country.

IN GRATEFUL ACKNOWLEDGMENT:

Grace Bostic for recipe preparation and testing
Viola Stroup and William Hansen for technical and editorial assistance.

CONTENTS

INTRODUCTION 9

HELPFUL HINTS 11

BASIC RECIPES & INGREDIENTS 13

EGG & CHEESE STUFFED SPUDS 25

FISH & SEAFOOD STUFFED SPUDS 45

POULTRY STUFFED SPUDS 69

MEAT STUFFED SPUDS 85

FRUIT & VEGETABLE STUFFED SPUDS 115

INDEX 133

INTRODUCTION

The potato is certainly the most widely used vegetable in the Western World and is often called the world's most important vegetable. The plant probably originated in the Andes, where it was cultivated by the Inca in pre-Columbian times. The Spanish conquistadors discovered the *papa*, which they called *patatas* and shipped back to Spain as ship's stores. The potato is considered by many to have been a more valuable find for the world than all of the silver in Peru.

Ironically, the potato of South America took almost a century to reach North America and arrived by a circuitous route – from Spain to Italy to Northern Europe to Bermuda to the Virginia colonies in 1621. However, the real importance of potato growing did not start until the Irish immigrants brought them to Londonderry, New Hampshire, in 1719.

Potatoes have also had a great impact on history. White potatoes became the major food source in Ireland in the nineteenth century and are therefore called Irish potatoes to distinguish them from sweet potatoes. In the potato blight in 1845, all of the potato plants all over Ireland turned black in the space of just a few weeks, and over a million Irish starved. The disease quickly spread to Europe. The Great Potato

Famine greatly altered the population of the United States, bringing thousands of Irish, Germans, and Poles to our shores.

Potato is the common name for a perennial plant (*Solanum tuberosum*) of the family *Solanaceae* (nigthshade family). It has a swollen underground stem or tuber. It grows best in a cool, moist climate. Most potatoes in the United States are now grown in Idaho, Washington, or Maine, although some are grown in all states.

Chemical analysis of the potato shows it to be high in potassium, phosphorus, and iron. It is also a good source of vitamin C and calcium. Most of the minerals and proteins are concentrated in a thin layer beneath the skin.

In today's weight-conscious society, potatoes are often regarded as "fattening," but they are not. One medium-size (eight-ounce) baked potato contains about 160 calories, less than the average serving of cottage cheese and fruit. However, the butter, sour cream, crumbled bacon, and other popular high-fat toppings are "fattening" whether served on a potato or by themselves. In fact potatoes are an ideal diet food because they are approximately 75% water and therefore very filling. Because they are also high in dietary fiber you are not apt to be hungry again for a long time.

The new wave of stuffed spud restaurants both in this country and in Europe prompted me to write this cookbook. A meal in a potato can be as simple or as elaborate as you wish. It can be the most economical approach to meal planning available or very expensive, depending on the ingredients you choose to put in it. A stuffed spud can also be a dieter's dream – very low in calories and very high in nutrition – or it can be a total debauchery.

The recipes in this book run the gamut. Read through the book, make your own choices and then your shopping list. Start having fun stuffing spuds!

HELPFUL HINTS

The potatoes recommended for baking are either the russets or the all-purpose potatoes found in your market. The term "Idaho" is reserved for russets grown in Idaho. The all-purpose potato resembles the russet in shape but has a thinner skin.

The recipes call for two potatoes, which will give you two servings. If you are counting calories, some of the recipes may look better to you if you make four servings instead of two. That way you can halve the "bottom line" nutritional information. Or, to serve more people, you can double, or triple the recipes as needed.

Although I used three-quarter-pound potatoes for developing the recipes, you can use half-pound potatoes. If smaller potatoes are used, you can use three instead of two.

When you cut the tops from baked potatoes, store these tops in a tightly sealed container in the freezer. Then when you want deep-fried potato skins you have them all ready to use. Also try brushing them with corn-oil margarine and putting them under the broiler until lightly browned and crisp. Serve broiled potato skins instead of toast, as cocktail food with a dip, or chop them up and use them as croutons in soups and salads.

Although all the recipes are for two potatoes, in a few recipes you only use the pulp from one potato. Store the unused pulp from the other potato in a tightly sealed container in the freezer to use later for potato pancakes or mashed, au gratin, or cottage-fried potatoes.

In a few of the recipes you will have more filling than will fit into the potato shells, even by heaping it up. The leftover filling makes a good filling for omelets or can be stored in the freezer for use as a vegetable side dish at another meal.

Almost all of the stuffed spuds to be served hot can be prepared ahead of time and then reheated just before serving. When reheating them, put them in a 350°F oven for 15 to 20 minutes. When making them ahead of time, do not garnish until after they have been reheated. Also, many of them are delicious cold and make wonderful school, work, or picnic lunches.

I have read in many books that you cannot successfully freeze potatoes; however I have found this not to be true. In testing these recipes, we have frozen all of them and find that the only recipes which cannot be frozen successfully are the salad-style recipes containing fresh vegetables such as tomatoes, lettuce, and cabbage. If you wish to freeze a salad-style recipe, do not add the shredded lettuce, cabbage, tomatoes, etc., until after the potato has thawed and you are ready to serve it. You will find that the reheated frozen stuffed spuds, whether taken directly from the freezer and reheated in a microwave oven for immediate serving, or thawed to room temperature and reheated in a conventional oven, are very good, perhaps not quite as good as they would have been before freezing, but certainly as good as the commercial TV dinners available at high prices in grocery stores. Create your own TV dinners; clean out the refrigerator and stuff some spuds, whether you're going to be home to eat them or not. Freeze them for future meals.

BASIC RECIPES
&
INGREDIENTS

Baked Potatoes

The following method is best for preparing potatoes for stuffing.

2 large baking potatoes

1. Preheat oven to 400°F. Wash the potatoes well and dry thoroughly. Pierce with the tines of a fork to keep the skins from bursting.

2. Bake for 1 hour.

3. Remove potatoes from the oven and allow to cool until comfortable to the touch.

If you rub potatoes with oil or margarine, or wrap them in foil, you soften the skins in the process. You want as tough-textured a potato shell as possible so it can be stuffed without tearing. I used ¾-pound potatoes for developing the recipes in this book.

I am also including two other interesting methods of preparation for baked potatoes which you may want to try.

Each potato contains approximately 160 calories, no cholesterol, negligible fat, 9 mg sodium.

Overbaked Potatoes

When I told James Beard about my working on this book, he asked me if I had ever eaten a potato baked at 450°F for 2 hours. I thought I had misunderstood him and asked again how long and at what temperature. He assured me that it was a perfectly wonderful way to serve a potato, unusual and delicious. He liked it served only with freshly ground black pepper. You may enjoy it in the James Beard style or you may prefer the more classic accompaniments, margarine and salt. The potato itself has a very thick crunchy outer shell, almost like a pastry crust. The inside has a rich, buttery consistency, which in my opinion really does not need butter or sour cream. I like it with fresh pepper and a little low-fat cottage cheese.

2 large baking potatoes

1. Preheat the oven to 450° F. Wash the potatoes well and dry thoroughly. Pierce them several times with the tines of a fork.

2. Place potatoes on the center rack of the preheated oven and bake for 2 hours.

3. Remove potatoes from the oven and cut lengthwise and then across the middle, almost through them. The shells will be very crisp and thick and will not squeeze easily. Open the potatoes and mash the inside pulp as best you can with a fork.

Nutritional information is the same as for Baked Potatoes, preceding.

Lined Potato "Bowls"

These lined potato "bowls" may be filled with any ingredients of your choice. They are convenient for serving leftovers of any type, such as chopped fish, poultry, or meat, cooked vegetables, even soups and salads.

2 baked potatoes
1 tablespoon corn-oil margarine or olive or canola oil
¼ cup nonfat milk
¼ teaspoon salt, or to taste
Freshly ground white or black pepper as desired

1. Cut a thin slice from the top of each potato. Remove the pulp from the potatoes, being careful not to tear the shells. Place the potato pulp in a mixing bowl and mash. Set the shells aside.

2. Add the margarine or oil, milk, and seasoning to taste to the potato pulp and mix thoroughly. Press through a sieve. Spoon the purée into the baked potato shells, pressing the mixture evenly over the entire inner surfaces with the back of a spoon.

Makes two servings.
Each serving contains approximately 246 calories, 1 mg cholesterol, 7 gm fat, 321 mg sodium.

Fifteen-Minute Chicken Stock

I call this Fifteen-Minute Chicken Stock because that is really all the time it takes in actual effort on your part. The rest of the time is simply letting the stock "do its own thing." After the chicken stock has cooked for an hour or more, you may want to throw in a whole chicken and cook it for your dinner or have it to dice for a salad or one of the fillings for your stuffed spuds. It will take the chicken less than an hour to cook, and overcooking can make it tough and dry; so as soon as it is tender, remove it from the stockpot.

3 to 5 pounds chicken bones, parts, and giblets, excluding liver
2 carrots, scraped and chopped
2 stalks celery, without leaves, chopped
1 onion, unpeeled, quartered
3 sprigs parsley
2 to 4 cloves garlic, unpeeled, halved
1 bay leaf
12 peppercorns
¼ cup white vinegar
Cold water to cover by 1 inch

1. Place all ingredients except the water in a large pot with a lid. Add the water and bring slowly to a boil over medium heat. Preparation up to this point takes about 5 minutes.

2. Reduce heat to low, cover, leaving lid ajar, and simmer for 3 hours or more. Longer cooking makes the stock more flavorful. Remove from heat and allow to stand until cool enough to handle. Remove and discard chicken parts and vegetables. Strain stock and allow to cool to room temperature. This step takes 5 minutes more. Refrigerate stock, uncovered, overnight or until fat has congealed on top.

3. Remove and discard fat; store stock in the freezer in containers of a volume you most often use. This step completes the 15 minutes of preparation time.

Makes approximately 10 cups.

Each 1-cup serving contains approximately negligible calories, cholesterol, and fat, and variable sodium.

Variation: TURKEY STOCK. Substitute 1 turkey carcass for chicken and use herbs and spices of your choice.

Beef Stock

With the exception of browning the bones and vegetables, beef stock should not take any more of your time than chicken stock to make. However, it should be allowed to simmer longer for extra-rich flavor, and you will occasionally need to skim off the foamy scum that will rise to the surface while the stock is cooking.

4 pounds beef or veal bones
3 large onions, with skin, cut into quarters
2 carrots, scraped and sliced
6 garlic cloves
4 parsley sprigs
2 whole cloves
1 teaspoon celery seeds
1 teaspoon dried thyme
1 teaspoon dried marjoram
2 bay leaves
$1/4$ teaspoon peppercorns
$1 1/2$ cups tomato juice (12-ounce can)
Defatted beef drippings (optional)
Water

1. Preheat the oven to 400°F. Brown the bones in a roasting pan for 30 minutes.

2. Add the onions, carrots, and garlic and brown together for another 30 minutes, or until ingredients are a rich, deep brown in color.

3. Put the browned meat and vegetables in a large pot or soup kettle with the remaining ingredients.

4. Add water to cover by 1 inch. Bring to a boil, then reduce heat and simmer for 5 minutes; remove any scum that forms on the top.

18

5. Cover, leaving the lid ajar about 1 inch to allow steam to escape, and simmer slowly for at least 5 hours; 10 hours are even better if you will be around to turn off the heat.

6. When the stock has finished cooking, allow it to come to room temperature. Refrigerate the stock, uncovered overnight.

7. When the fat has hardened on the surface of the stock, remove it. Warm the defatted stock until it becomes liquid.

8. Strain the liquid and taste. If the flavor of the stock is too weak, boil it down to evaporate more of the liquid and concentrate its strength.

9. Store the stock in the freezer in the size containers you will be using most frequently. You can then take the stock directly from the freezer and melt it whenever you need it.

Makes about 10 cups.
Each 1-cup serving contains negligible calories, cholesterol, and fat, and variable sodium.

Fish Stock

2 pounds fish heads, bones, and trimmings
2½ quarts water
3 onions, peeled and sliced
6 parsley sprigs
1 carrot, scraped and sliced
1 teaspoon dried marjoram
¼ teaspoon peppercorns
¼ cup freshly squeezed lemon juice

1. Bring all ingredients to a boil and simmer, uncovered, for about 45 minutes.

2. Line a colander or strainer with damp cheesecloth and strain the fish stock through it.

3. Cool to room temperature and store in the refrigerator. If you are not planning to use the fish stock within 2 days, store it in the freezer.

Makes 8 cups stock.
Each 1-cup serving contains negligible calories, cholesterol, and fat, and variable sodium.

White Sauce

1 cup low-fat milk
2 tablespoons corn-oil margarine
1½ tablespoons sifted unbleached all-purpose flour
⅛ teaspoon salt

1. Put the milk in a saucepan on low heat and bring to the boiling point.

2. In another saucepan, melt the margarine over medium heat and add the flour, stirring constantly. Cook, stirring, for 3 minutes. DO NOT BROWN.

3. Remove the flour and margarine mixture from the heat and add the simmering milk all at once, stirring constantly with a wire whisk.

4. Put the sauce back on low heat and cook slowly until thickened, stirring occasionally.

5. Add the salt and mix thoroughly. If there are lumps in the sauce, process it in a blender container until smooth.

Makes 1 cup.
Each ½-cup serving contains approximately 185 calories, 9 mg cholesterol, 14 gm fat, 346 mg sodium.

Hollandaise Sauce

2 egg yolks
2 tablespoons freshly squeezed lemon juice
1/8 teaspoon salt
Pinch cayenne pepper
6 tablespoons corn-oil margarine, melted
3 egg whites
1/8 teaspoon cream of tartar

1. Place egg yolks, lemon juice, salt, and cayenne pepper in a blender container. Cover the blender and blend at high speed 2 to 3 seconds. Reduce speed to medium. Remove the lid but leave the blender running and slowly pour in melted margarine in a very thin stream. Set aside. (If you are not going to use the sauce immediately, set the blender container into a pan of lukewarm water so that the sauce will not separate.)

2. Combine egg whites and cream of tartar and beat until soft peaks form. Gradually fold sauce mixture into egg whites until it is smooth but still a very light mixture. Use immediately!

Makes 3 cups.
Each 1/4-cup serving contains approximately 66 calories, 36 mg cholesterol, 7 gm fat, 118 mg sodium.

Pizza Sauce

1 medium onion, finely chopped (1½ cups)
2 garlic cloves, pressed or peeled and minced (2 teaspoons)
¼ cup finely chopped parsley
2 tablespoons water
2 (6-ounce) cans tomato paste (1½ cups)
1 teaspoon dried oregano, crushed in a mortar using a pestle
½ teaspoon dried basil, crushed in a mortar using a pestle
½ teaspoon salt
¼ teaspoon freshly ground black pepper

1. Combine onion, garlic, parsley, and water in a saucepan and cook, covered, until soft, about 8 minutes.

2. Add all remaining ingredients and mix well. If not using immediately, remove from heat and allow to cool to room temperature. Store, tightly covered, in the refrigerator.

Makes about 2 cups.
Each ½-cup serving contains approximately 110 calories, no cholesterol, 1 gm fat, 1087 mg sodium.

Jet Fuel Dressing

½ cup red wine vinegar
½ teaspoon salt
1 tablespoon fructose
¼ teaspoon freshly ground black pepper
2 tablespoons freshly squeezed lemon juice
2 teaspoons reduced-sodium Worcestershire sauce
1 tablespoon Dijon-style mustard
2 cloves garlic, minced
1 cup water
2 tablespoons canola oil (optional)

1. Dissolve salt in the vinegar. Add all other ingredients and mix well. Store in the refrigerator in a jar with a tight-fitting lid. Shake well before each use.

Makes 2 cups.
Each 2-tablespoon serving contains approximately 5 calories, no cholesterol, negligible fat, 85 mg sodium.

Variations: CUMIN. Add ½ teaspoon ground cumin to Jet Fuel Dressing; mix thoroughly.

CURRY. Add 1 teaspoon curry powder to Jet Fuel Dressing; mix thoroughly.

ITALIAN. Add 2 teaspoons dried oregano and 1 teaspoon each dried basil and dried tarragon, crushed, to Jet Fuel Dressing; mix thoroughly.

TARRAGON. Add 1 tablespoon dried taragon, crushed, to Jet Fuel Dressing; mix thoroughly.

On Stocks, Sauces, & Salad Dressing

As the recipes in this chapter show, it is relatively easy to prepare your own stocks, sauces, and dressing. They do make a big difference in the flavor of dishes, and they are less expensive. Canned or bottled products may also be used, of course. Prepared chicken or beef stock is often sold as chicken broth or beef broth and can be defatted the same way you defat homemade stock in your refrigerator.

On Fructose

I use pure crystalline fructose, a kind of sugar, in these recipes because it is sweeter than ordinary table sugar, so less of it is needed. It serves to heighten and sharpen flavors, especially in the absence of salt. It is available in the dietetic section of your market or in health food stores. You may use sugar anytime fructose is called for, but you will need to increase the amount by one-half to have similar results.

EGG & CHEESE STUFFED SPUDS

Many of the egg and cheese stuffed spuds are wonderful for brunch entrees. If you are entertaining, they are also practical for buffets because they are one-dish meals. One of my favorite brunch menus is Spud "Crepes" Florentine served with sliced melon.

These recipes are also excellent budget stretchers as meatless meals for any occasion. Surprise your friends with Pizza Potatoes and a tossed green salad with Italian dressing the next time you are having guests for dinner.

Most of these recipes are good for vegetarian meal planning. A very few of them call for chicken stock. The Runner's Stuffed Spud is a great "brown bag" lunch for vegetarian menus.

Eggs Foo Yung Spud

For an unusual approach to an oriental dinner, serve this spud as the entree with stir-fried pea pods. Have egg-flower soup to start and fortune cookies for dessert.

2 baked potatoes
Sauce:
    1 tablespoon sodium-reduced soy sauce
    2 teaspoons cornstarch
    1 tablespoon rice vinegar
    1/2 cup water
    1 teaspoon fructose
1 tablespoon canola oil
1 egg plus 2 egg whites, lightly beaten, OR
    1/2 cup liquid egg substitute
1/4 teaspoon salt
1/2 cup bean sprouts
1/4 cup finely chopped green onion tops

1. Cut a thin slice from the top of each potato. Remove the pulp from the potatoes, being careful not to tear the shells. Place the potato pulp in a mixing bowl and mash; cover and set aside. Keep the shells warm.

2. Combine the sauce ingredients and cook over low heat, stirring constantly until thickened (or you may warm 1/4 cup of any commercial sweet-and-sour sauce). Keep sauce warm.

3. Heat the oil in a skillet over medium heat. Add the eggs, salt, bean sprouts, green onion tops, and mashed potatoes and cook until set, like scrambled eggs.

4. Heap the egg mixture into the warm potato shells and pour the sauce over the top.

Makes two servings.
Each serving contains approximately 332 calories, 107 mg cholesterol, 10 gm fat, 691 mg sodium.

Vegetarian Quiche Spud

2 baked potatoes
1 tablespoon corn-oil margarine
¼ cup chopped onion
½ cup light sour cream
1 egg plus 2 egg whites, lightly beaten, OR
    ½ cup liquid egg substitute
⅛ teaspoon salt
⅛ teaspoon freshly ground black pepper
¾ cup ¼-inch cubes 20% fat-reduced Swiss cheese
1 cup chopped assorted cooked leftover vegetables
Chopped parsley, for garnish

1. Cut a thin slice from the top of each potato. Remove the pulp from the potatoes, being careful not to tear the shells. Place the potato pulp in a mixing bowl and mash; cover and set aside. Set the shells aside.

2. Heat the margarine in a skillet. Add the onion and cook over low heat until tender, about 10 minutes. Add the sour cream, lightly beaten eggs, salt, and pepper, stirring constantly. Add the mashed potatoes and mix well. Add the cheese and assorted cooked vegetables and mix lightly.

3. Heap the mixture into the potato shells. Bake at 350°F for 45 minutes. Garnish with chopped parsley just before serving.

Makes two servings.
Each serving contains approximately 462 calories, 152 mg cholesterol, 20 mg fat, 388 mg sodium.

Variation: Substitute ½ cup cooked tempeh for ½ cup of the chopped vegetables.

Potato-Cheese Soufflé in Spuds

2 baked potatoes
½ cup low-fat milk, at the boiling point
2 tablespoons corn-oil margarine
1 tablespoon unbleached all-purpose flour
1 egg yolk
½ cup grated 20% fat-reduced sharp cheddar cheese
¼ teaspoon salt
Pinch of white pepper
3 egg whites
⅛ teaspoon cream of tartar

1.   Cut a thin slice from the top of each potato. Remove the pulp from the potatoes, being careful not to tear the shells. Place the potato pulp in a mixing bowl and mash; cover and set aside. Spread the shells out as liners in 4-inch oven-proof bowls or soufflé dishes.

2.   Preheat the oven to 400°F. Pour the milk into a small saucepan over low heat. Melt the margarine in another saucepan. Add the flour to the melted margarine, stirring constantly for 3 minutes. DO NOT BROWN!

3.   Take the flour mixture off the heat and pour in the boiling milk all at once, stirring constantly with a wire whisk. Put the pan back on the heat and allow sauce to come to a boil, stirring constantly. Boil for 1 minute. Remove from the heat and add the egg yolk, stirring in thoroughly.

4.   Add the cheese and mix thoroughly. Add salt, pepper, and Worcestershire sauce. Add ¾ cup of the mashed potato and mix thoroughly. (Store the remaining mashed potato for another meal.)

5.   Combine the egg whites and cream of tartar and beat until stiff but not dry. Add one quarter of the egg whites to the potato-cheese mixture and stir them in. Add remaining egg whites and carefully fold them in, being sure not to over mix.

6. Spoon the mixture into the potato shells in the bowls or soufflé dishes and place in the preheated oven. Immediately turn the oven down to 375°F and bake for 15 to 20 minutes. Serve immediately. Remember the old saying: "It is better to wait for a soufflé because a soufflé will not wait for you."

Makes two servings.
Each serving contains approximately 375 calories, 135 mg cholesterol, 23 gm fat, 554 mg sodium.

Tofu Stuffed Spud

2 baked potatoes
1 cup silken soft tofu (8 ounces)
1 egg, lightly beaten
1 teaspoon seasoned salt
½ cup chopped green onions
½ cup light sour cream
½ cup grated 20% fat-reduced cheddar cheese

1. Cut a thin slice from the top of each potato. Remove the pulp from the potatoes, being careful not to tear the shells. Keep the shells warm. Place the potato pulp and tofu in a mixing bowl and mash together until thoroughly mixed.

2. Combine the beaten egg and seasoned salt and add to the potato-tofu mixture; mix well. Add all other ingredients and mix well.

3. Heap into the warm potato shells and bake at 350°F for 45 minutes.

Makes two servings.
Each serving contains approximately 477 calories, 154 mg cholesterol, 23 gm fat, 664 mg sodium.

Banana Breakfast Spud

This is also a nutritious after-school snack or an unusual light supper entree.

2 baked potatoes
1 cup low-fat ricotta or cottage cheese
2 tablespoons fructose
1½ teaspoons vanilla extract
1 teaspoon freshly grated lemon rind
1 teaspoon freshly squeezed lemon juice
2 ripe bananas, mashed
Ground cinnamon, for garnish (optional)
Cinnamon sticks, for garnish (optional)

1. Cut the potatoes into halves and let them cool to room temperature. Remove the potato pulp, being careful not to tear the shells.

2. Place the potato pulp and all other ingredients except the garnish in a blender container and blend until smooth.

3. Spoon the mixture into the potato shells and garnish with ground cinnamon. Place a cinnamon stick in each potato half.

Makes 2 servings.
Each serving contains approximately 484 calories, 38 mg cholesterol, 10 gm fat, 166 mg sodium.

Runner's Stuffed Spud

The Runner's Stuffed Spud is a wonderful pick-me-up for marathon runners or just beginning joggers to have on returning home. It is good for breakfast, lunch, dinner, or just a high-energy snack.

2 tablespoons sunflower seeds
2 baked potatoes
¼ cup nonfat milk
2 tablespoons honey
½ cup low-fat cottage cheese
1 apple, finely chopped
¼ cup raisins
½ teaspoon ground cinnamon
1 teaspoon vanilla extract

1. Toast the sunflower seeds on the center rack of a 350°F oven for 8 to 10 minutes, or until golden brown. Watch them carefully as they burn easily. Set aside.

2. Cut a thin slice from the top of each potato. Remove the pulp from the potatoes, being careful not to tear the shells. Place the potato pulp in a mixing bowl, add the milk and honey and mash thoroughly.

3. Add the remaining ingredients, including the toasted sunflower seeds, and mix well.

4. Heap the mixture into the potato shells. Serve immediately or refrigerate until cold.

Makes two servings.
Each serving contains approximately 437 calories, 3 mg cholesterol, 5 gm fat, 258 mg sodium.

Canyon Ranch Stuft Spud

This potato is a popular luncheon entrée at the Canyon Ranch Vacation Fitness Resorts in both Tucson, Arizona, and Lenox, Massachusetts.

2 small baked potatoes
1 medium onion, finely chopped
¼ cup buttermilk
½ cup low-fat cottage cheese
3 tablespoons freshly grated Parmesan cheese
2 tablespoons chopped chives or green onion tops

1. Cut a thin slice from the top of each potato. Remove the pulp from the potatoes, being careful not to tear the shells. Place the potato pulp in a mixing bowl and mash; cover and set aside. Keep the shells warm.

2. Cook the onion, covered, over very low heat until soft, stirring occasionally and adding a little water if necessary to prevent scorching. Add the mashed potatoes, buttermilk, cottage cheese and all other ingredients except the chopped green onions. Mix well and heat thoroughly.

3. Stuff the potato mixture back into the warm shells. The mixture will be heaping way over the top.

4. To serve, sprinkle the top of each Stuft Spud with 1 tablespoon chopped chives or green onion tops. If you have prepared them in advance, heat in a 350°F oven for 10 to 15 minutes, or until hot, before adding the chopped onions.

Makes 2 servings.
Each serving contains approximately 342 calories, 12 mg cholesterol, 3 gm fat, 419 mg sodium.

Potato Primavera Spud

The inspiration for Potato Primavera Spud obviously came from Pasta Primavera and you will be surprised to find you may like it even better.

2 tablespoons pine nuts
2 baked potatoes
½ cup white sauce (see Index)
⅛ teaspoon salt
¼ cup freshly grated Parmesan cheese
¼ cup cooked peas
¼ cup diced cooked carrots
¼ cup diced cooked yellow squash
¼ cup cooked small broccoli flowerets
½ cup cooked chopped onion
1 small tomato, peeled and diced, for garnish

1. Toast the pine nuts in a 350°F oven for 8 to 10 minutes, or until golden brown. Watch them carefully as they burn easily. Set aside.

2. Cut a thin slice from the top of each potato. Remove the pulp from the potatoes, being careful not to tear the shells. Keep the shells warm.

3. Crumble the potato pulp. Add the white sauce, salt, and Parmesan cheese and mix thoroughly. Add all other vegetables except the tomatoes and mix well. Add the pine nuts and mix thoroughly.

4. Heap into the warm potato shells. Garnish each potato with some diced tomato.

Makes two servings.
Each serving contains approximately 416 calories, 12 mg cholesterol, 16 gm fat, 656 mg sodium.

Variations: You may vary the vegetables according to what you have on hand. It is best to have a colorful combination, all cooked just crisp-tender. You may either heat the white sauce and the vegetables before adding them to the crumbled potato pulp, or add them cold and put the stuffed potato in a 350°F oven for 10 to 15 minutes before garnishing with the tomato.

33

Vegetable Stuffed Spud

2 baked potatoes
½ cup white sauce (see Index)
¼ teaspoon salt
½ cup grated 20% fat-reduced Monterey Jack cheese
¼ cup cooked peas (if frozen, thaw first)
¼ cup chopped cooked carrots
2 tablespoons chopped green bell pepper
1 tablespoon diced pimiento

1. Cut the baked potatoes into halves. Scoop out the pulp, mash well, and set aside in a covered bowl.

2. Combine all other ingredients and mix well. Stir into the mashed potato and again mix well.

3. Heap the mixture into the potato halves. Place them on an ungreased cookie sheet, and bake in a 375°F oven for 20 to 25 minutes, or until the tops are brown.

Makes two servings.
Each serving contains approximately 345 calories, 20 mg cholesterol, 10 gm fat, 546 mg sodium.

Beer & Pretzel Spud

This speedy spud can be made in minutes and enjoyed with the rest of the can of cold beer while watching Monday night football.

2 baked potatoes
⅓ cup beer, your favorite brand
¼ cup grated 20% fat-reduced sharp cheddar cheese
¼ teaspoon salt
Pretzel sticks, for garnish

1. Cut a thin slice from the top of each potato. Remove the pulp from the potatoes, being careful not to tear the shells. Place the potato pulp in a mixing bowl and mash; cover and set aside. Keep the shells warm.

2. Combine the beer and the cheese in a saucepan and cook over low heat until the cheese is completely melted. Add the mashed potato and salt and mix thoroughly, stirring constantly until the mixture is heated through.

3. Heap the mixture into the warm potato shells and garnish with broken pretzel sticks.

Makes two servings.
Each serving contains approximately 227 calories, 12 mg cholesterol, 4 gm fat, 356 mg sodium.

Rarebit in a Spud

2 baked potatoes
½ teaspoon Dijon-style mustard
½ teaspoon Worcestershire sauce
½ teaspoon curry powder
⅛ teaspoon caraway seed
⅛ teaspoon salt
⅛ teaspoon freshly ground black pepper
Pinch paprika
3 tablespoons ale
2 dashes Tabasco (or to taste)
1⅓ cup grated 20% fat-reduced sharp cheddar cheese
2 tablespoons sliced ripe olives
2 tablespoons pimiento strips
Chopped parsley, for garnish

1. Cut a thin slice from the top of each potato. Remove the pulp from the potatoes, being careful not to tear the shells. Place the potato pulp in a mixing bowl and mash; cover and set aside. Keep the shells warm.

2. In the top of a double boiler, combine the mustard, Worcestershire sauce, curry powder, caraway seed, salt, pepper, paprika, ale, and Tabasco. Mix well and heat over gently boiling water.

3. Reduce heat to medium-low and gradually add cheese to spice-and-ale mixture, whisking constantly until all cheese is melted and mixture is hot. Add the mashed potato pulp, mixing well. Add the olives and pimiento, stir lightly and heat through.

4. Heap the mixture into the warm potato shells and garnish with chopped parsley.

Makes two servings.
Each serving contains approximately 427 calories, 60 mg cholesterol, 19 gm fat, 508 mg sodium.

Potato & Onion au Gratin

2 baked potatoes
1 teaspoon canola oil
2 medium onions, finely chopped
½ cup grated Gruyère or 20% fat-reduced Swiss cheese

1. Cut a thin slice from the top of each potato. Remove the pulp from the potatoes, being careful not to tear the shells. Place the potato pulp in a mixing bowl and mash; cover and set aside. Keep the shells warm.

2. Warm the oil in a skillet over low heat. Sauté the onions, covered, until clear and soft, about 10 minutes. Stir occasionally and add water if necessary to prevent scorching.

3. Uncover and sauté onions until browned, about 20 minutes, stirring occasionally to assure even browning.

4. Combine the onions and potato pulp and mix thoroughly. Spoon the potato mixture into the warm potato "bowls" and top each with ¼ cup of the grated cheese.

5. Bake in a 375°F oven for 20 minutes, or until the cheese is lightly browned.

Makes two servings.
Each serving contains approximately 330 calories, 15 mg cholesterol, 6 gm fat, 49 mg sodium.

Spud "Crepes" Florentine

2 baked potatoes
1/2 cup low-fat ricotta cheese
1/4 cup nonfat milk
1 garlic clove, minced or pressed
1/8 teaspoon salt
1 cup chopped cooked drained spinach (1 pound raw)
2 tablespoons freshly grated Parmesan cheese

1. Cut a thin slice from the top of each potato. Remove the pulp from the potatoes, being careful not to tear the shells. Place the potato pulp in a mixing bowl and mash; cover and set aside. Keep the shells warm.

2. Add the cheese, milk, garlic, and salt to the mashed potatoes and mix well. Add the spinach and again mix well.

3. Heap the mixture into the warm potato shells and top with Parmesan cheese. Bake in a 350°F oven for 20 minutes.

Makes two servings.
Each serving contains approximately 314 calories, 23 mg cholesterol, 7 gm fat, 400 mg sodium.

Enchildadas de Papas

(Potato Enchiladas)

Enchiladas de Papas may be the next Mexican classic. If you don't
have any tortillas and you feel like eating an enchilada, you will find
Enchiladas de Papas *fantástico*!

2 baked potatoes
1 tablespoon corn oil
1 small onion, finely chopped
½ teaspoon salt
¼ teaspoon ground cumin seed
1 teaspoon chili powder
¼ cup chicken stock (see Index)
1 large tomato, peeled and diced
½ cup grated 20% fat-reduced cheddar cheese

1. Cut a thin slice from the top of each potato. Remove the pulp
from the potatoes, being careful not to tear the shells. Place the potato
pulp in a mixing bowl and mash; cover and set aside. Keep the shells
warm.

2. Heat the oil in a skillet. Add the chopped onion and cook over
low heat until clear and soft, about 10 minutes.

3. Add the salt, cumin seed, chili powder, and chicken stock and
mix well. Add the tomato and mashed potato and mix well. Cook over
low heat for 5 minutes. Add ¼ cup of the cheese and mix thoroughly,
heating through.

4. Heap the enchilada filling into the warm potato shells. Sprinkle
the top of each potato with 2 tablespoons of grated cheese. Bake in
a 350°F oven until the cheese is melted.

Makes two servings.
Each serving contains approximately 368 calories, 24 mg cholesterol,
15 gm fat, 729 mg sodium.

Papas Refritos con Queso

(Refried Potatoes with Cheese)

2 baked potatoes
1 tablespoon corn oil
1 small onion
2 garlic cloves, minced or pressed
2 teaspoons chili powder
1/4 teaspoon salt
1/2 cup tomato sauce
Dash of Tabasco (optional)
1 cup grated 20% fat-reduced sharp cheddar or Monterey Jack cheese

1. Cut a thin slice from the top of each potato. Remove the pulp from the potatoes, being careful not to tear the shells. Place the potato pulp in a mixing bowl and mash; cover and set aside. Keep the shells warm.

2. Heat the oil in a skillet. Add the onion and garlic, and cook over low heat until soft, about 10 minutes. Add the chili powder and salt, and mix well.

3. Add the mashed potatoes to the skillet mixture and mix thoroughly. Cook, stirring frequently, for 5 minutes.

4. Add the tomato sauce, Tabasco, and 3/4 cup of the cheese; mix well.

5. Heap the "refried" potatoes into the shells and top each potato with 2 tablespoons of grated cheese. Bake in a 350°F oven for 5 minutes, or until the cheese has melted.

Makes two servings.
Each serving contains approximately 372 calories, 20 mg cholesterol, 14 gm fat, 867 mg sodium.

Variation: BEAN BURRITO SPUD. Add 1 cup mashed cooked pinto beans in step 3 with the mashed potatoes.

Pizza Potato

After having Pizza Potato you may be spoiled forever for regular pizza.

2 baked potatoes
4 teaspoons extra-virgin olive oil
2 teaspoons freshly grated Parmesan cheese
1 teaspoon oregano, crushed in a mortar with a pestle
Salt
Pepper
1 cup Pizza Sauce (see Index)
1 cup grated part-skim mozzarella cheese

1. Cut the potatoes into halves lengthwise. Using a knife, cut slits about ½ inch apart in the edges of the potato shells and flatten the potato halves to form the bases for the other ingredients. Place shells on a cookie sheet.

2. Using a fork, work 1 teaspoon oil, ½ teaspoon Parmesan cheese, ¼ teaspoon oregano, and pinches of salt and pepper into the potato pulp of each "pizza" base. Spread ¼ cup pizza sauce on top of each base, and top with ¼ cup grated cheese.

3. Bake in a 400°F oven for 10 to 15 minutes, or until the cheese is completely melted. If you wish your pizza lightly browned, put it under the broiler for 2 minutes before serving.

Makes two servings.
Each serving contains approximately 517 calories, 34 mg cholesterol, 20 gm fat, 1685 mg sodium.

Variations: Add thin slices of pepperoni or sausage, anchovies, mushrooms, green pepper, or any other topping you particularly like on pizza, on top of the cheese. You can use canned pizza sauce if you're in a hurry.

Potato Relleno

Potato Relleno was inspired by the classic Mexican dish, Chile Relleno, and it is equally delicious.

2 baked potatoes
¼ cup chicken stock (see Index)
1 cup grated 20% fat-reduced Monterey Jack cheese
1 (4-ounce) can Ortega chiles, seeds removed and chopped
¼ teaspoon salt
½ teaspoon ground cumin seed
1 egg, separated

1. Slit the tops of the potatoes and carefully remove the pulp. Keep the potato shells warm.

2. Mash the potato pulp and add the chicken stock, grated cheese, chopped chiles, salt, and cumin seed; mix thoroughly.

3. Stuff the mixture into the baked potato shells, and press potatoes closed. Bake in a preheated 400° F oven for 10 minutes, or until the cheese is completely melted.

4. Beat the egg white until stiff but not dry. Beat the egg yolk until smooth and fold the yolk into the egg white. Spoon half of the egg mixture over the top of each potato.

5. Place the potatoes under the broiler until lightly browned.

Makes two servings.
Each serving contains approximately 387 calories, 147 mg cholesterol, 15 gm fat, 1323 mg sodium.

Variations: POTATO CHICKEN RELLENO. Add 1 cup chopped cooked chicken in step 2.

VEGETARIAN "CHICKEN" RELLENO. Add ½ cup cooked tempeh in step 2.

42

Northern Italian Stuffed Spud

2 baked potatoes
1 tablespoon extra-virgin olive oil
1 small onion, finely chopped
1 small carrot, scraped and finely chopped
2 tablespoons finely chopped parsley
¼ cup dry white wine
½ teaspoon salt
⅛ teaspoon white pepper
¼ teaspoon oregano, crushed in a mortar with a pestle
¼ teaspoon basil, crushed in a mortar with a pestle
½ cup white sauce (see Index)
2 tablespoons freshly grated Parmesan cheese
⅛ teaspoon grated nutmeg
Chopped parsley, for garnish (optional)

1. Cut a thin slice from the top of each potato. Remove the pulp from the potatoes, being careful not to tear the shells. Place the potato pulp in a mixing bowl and mash; cover and set aside. Keep the shells warm.

2. Heat the oil in a skillet. Add the onion, carrot, and parsley and cook over low heat until tender, about 10 minutes.

3. Combine the wine, seasoning, and herbs, and add to the vegetables. Simmer until the wine is completely absorbed. Remove from the heat.

4. Combine the white sauce, Parmesan cheese, and nutmeg, and mix well. Combine the white sauce mixture, crumbled potatoes, and cooked vegetables, and mix well. Place back on the heat until heated through.

5. Heap the mixture into the warm potato shells. Garnish with chopped parsley.

Makes two servings.

Each serving contains approximately 393 calories, 8 mg cholesterol, 16 gm fat, 873 mg sodium.

Variation: SWEETBREAD STUFFED SPUD. Add ½ cup chopped cooked veal sweetbread to the mixture in step 4.

FISH & SEAFOOD STUFFED SPUDS

Fish and seafood stuffed spuds are delightfully different. Many people who aren't crazy about fish will be pleasantly surprised at how good the combination of potatoes and all types of fish and seafood is.

The Shrimp Salad in a Spud is a superb luncheon entrée and certainly an unusual approach to potato salad.

The Dilled Fish Stuffed Spud Amandine is my favorite recipe for using leftover fish and is also a good entrée for buffets because it is so easy to serve.

Dilled Fish Stuffed Spud Amandine

2 tablespoons chopped raw almonds
2 baked potatoes
¼ cup nonfat, cholesterol-free mayonnaise dressing
½ cup light sour cream
¼ teaspoon salt
¼ teaspoon tarragon, crushed in a mortar with a pestle
½ teaspoon dried dill weed, crushed in a mortar with a pestle
¾ cup chopped cooked fish (any leftover fish will do)

1. Toast the almonds in a 350°F oven for 8 to 10 minutes, or until golden brown. Watch them carefully as they burn easily. Set aside.

2. Cut a thin slice from the top of each potato. Remove the pulp from the potatoes, being careful not to tear the shells. Place the potato pulp in a mixing bowl and mash. Keep the shells warm.

3. Add the mayonnaise, sour cream, salt, tarragon, and dill weed to the mashed potatoes and mix thoroughly. Add the fish and toasted almonds, reserving enough of the almonds to sprinkle over the tops for garnish.

4. Heap the mixture into the potato shells. Heat in a 350°F oven for 15 minutes. Garnish with the reserved almonds before serving.

Makes two servings.
Each serving contains approximately 440 calories, 63 mg cholesterol, 13 gm fat, 760 mg sodium.

Variations: CHICKEN WITH DILL SAUCE IN A SPUD. Substitute 2 tablespoons sunflower seeds for the almonds (toasted the same way), and ¾ cup chopped cooked chicken for the fish; garnish with fresh dill if available.

VEGETARIAN "CHICKEN" WITH DILL SAUCE IN A SPUD. Substitute ½ cup cooked tempeh for the chopped chicken in the first variation.

Fish Véronique Stuffed Spud

2 baked potatoes
½ cup white sauce (see Index)
2 tablespoons sherry
¾ cup chopped cooked firm white fish
½ pound seedless grapes, OR
   1 (8 ½-ounce) can, drained
⅛ teaspoon salt
⅛ teaspoon white pepper
Seedless grapes, for garnish

1.   Cut a thin slice from the top of each potato. Remove the pulp from the potatoes, being careful not to tear the shells. Place the potato pulp in a mixing bowl. Set the shells aside.

2.   Add the white sauce and sherry to the potato pulp and mash thoroughly.

3.   Add the fish, grapes, salt, and pepper to the potato mixture and mix well. Heap the mixture into the potato shells and heat in a 350°F oven for 15 minutes. Garnish with seedless grapes.

Makes two servings.
Each serving contains approximately 442 calories, 45 mg cholesterol, 9 gm fat, 387 mg sodium.

Variation: CHICKEN VÉRONIQUE STUFFED SPUD. Substitute ¾ cup chopped cooked chicken for the chopped fish.

47

Bouillabaisse Stuffed Spud

Marseilles, on the south coast of France, is the undisputed bouillabaisse capital of the world; however, there is a great difference of opinion as to what ingredients are essential to make it "authentic." Around Marseilles you won't find shellfish in bouillabaisse, so this Bouillabaisse Stuffed Spud is at least half authentic. They serve theirs with crusty bread and this one is served in a spud.

¼ pound fresh white fish
2 teaspoons freshly squeezed lemon juice
1 tablespoon extra-virgin olive oil
1 small onion, thinly sliced
¼ cup chopped leek, white part only
1 garlic clove, finely chopped
1 tomato, peeled, seeded, and diced
1 tablespoon chopped parsley
¼ cup chopped celery
1 bay leaf
½ teaspoon salt
⅛ teaspoon ground fennel seed
⅛ teaspoon dried thyme
⅛ teaspoon ground saffron
Pinch of freshly ground black pepper
½ cup chicken stock or fish stock (see Index)
1 cup dry white wine
Parsley sprigs, for garnish (optional)

1. Wash the fish in cold water and pat dry. Cut into bite-size pieces. Sprinkle with lemon juice and salt lightly. Set aside.

2. Cut a thin slice from the top of each potato. Remove the pulp from the potatoes, being careful not to tear the shells. Crumble the potato pulp and cover. Keep the shells warm.

3. Heat the oil in a skillet. Add the vegetables, herbs, and seasonings; mix thoroughly. Cook over low heat for 3 minutes. Add the stock and wine and bring to a boil. Simmer for 10 more minutes, reducing the liquid by half.

4. Add the fish and continue to boil until the fish has turned white, about 5 minutes. Remove the bay leaf and add the crumbled potato pulp. Mix thoroughly and heap into the warm potato shells.

Makes two servings.
Each serving contains approximately 490 calories, 66 mg cholesterol, 10 gm fat, 758 mg sodium.

Classic Caviar Spud

This is a glamorous entrée to serve on your yacht, at the beach house, or at your weekend hideaway in the mountains. It is simple to prepare and all of the ingredients can be easily packed to take with you. Also, it takes very little kitchen space for preparation. It can also be an elegant entrée for a candlelight dinner for two, served with a cold watercress salad, fruit marinated in Grand Marnier for dessert, and of course a bottle of chilled champagne.

2 baked potatoes
1 cup light sour cream
2 hard-cooked egg whites, finely chopped
¼ cup finely chopped onion
2 ounces red caviar
Watercress, for garnish (optional)

1. Cut a thin slice from the top of each potato. Remove the pulp from the potatoes, being careful not to tear the shells.

2. Combine potato pulp and sour cream and mash well. Add chopped egg white and onion and mix thoroughly.

3. Heap the potato mixture in the potato shells and top each potato with 2 tablespoons of caviar. The Classic Caviar Spud is good served hot or cold. Garnish with watercress if desired.

Serves two.
Each serving contains approximately 430 calories, 213 mg cholesterol, 20 gm fat, 535 mg sodium.

Crab & Swiss Cheese Spud

2 tablespoons slivered almonds
2 baked potatoes
1 tablespoon canola oil
¼ cup sliced green onions
1 teaspoon dry mustard
1 teaspoon grated lemon rind
½ cup grated 20% fat-reduced Swiss cheese
Pinch of ground mace
½ teaspoon salt
⅛ teaspoon freshly ground black pepper
½ cup nonfat milk
¾ cup chopped fresh crab meat
Chopped parsley, for garnish
Chopped pimiento, for garnish (optional)

1. Toast the almonds in a 350°F oven for 8 to 10 minutes, or until golden brown. Watch them carefully as they burn easily. Set aside.

2. Cut a thin slice from the top of each potato. Remove the pulp from the potatoes, being careful not to tear the shells. Place the potato pulp in a mixing bowl and mash; cover and set aside. Keep the shells warm.

3. Heat the oil in a skillet. Add the onions and cook until tender, about 10 minutes.

4. Combine the mustard, lemon rind, grated cheese, mace, salt, and pepper and set aside. Heat the milk; add it to the mashed potatoes and mix thoroughly.

5. Add the potato mixture and the cheese mixture to the onions in the skillet, stirring lightly until the cheese is melted and the mixture is thoroughly heated.

6. Add the crab meat and almonds and stir until the crab meat is heated. Heap the mixture into the warm potato shells. Garnish with parsley or pimiento or both.

Makes two servings.
Each serving contains approximately 460 calories, 98 mg cholesterol, 16 gm fat, 977 mg sodium.

Variation: Instead of fresh crab, use 6 ounces canned crab meat, flaked. In step 6, do not stir vigorously or crab will become mushy.

Curried Crab in Spuds

2 baked potatoes
1 tablespoon corn-oil margarine
½ cup chopped onion
¼ cup nonfat, cholesterol-free mayonnaise dressing
¼ cup light sour cream
1½ teaspoons curry powder
½ teaspoon salt
⅛ teaspoon ground ginger
½ cup crushed pineapple, packed in juice, drained
¾ cup diced fresh crab meat, OR
    1 (6-ounce) can, drained, rinsed under cold water, drained again thoroughly, and flaked

1. Cut a thin slice from the top of each potato. Remove the pulp from the potatoes, being careful not to tear the shells. Place the potato pulp in a mixing bowl and crumble; cover and set aside. Keep the shells warm.

2. Heat the margarine in a large skillet. Add the onion and cook over low heat until tender, about 10 minutes.

3. Combine the mayonnaise, sour cream, curry powder, salt, and ginger and mix well. Stir the mayonnaise mixture into the potatoes.

4. Combine all ingredients in the skillet, mix well, and heat through. Heap the mixture into the warm potato shells and serve immediately.

Makes two servings.
Each serving contains approximately 440 calories, 88 mg cholesterol, 12 gm fat, 1279 mg sodium.

Spud Oscar

2 baked potatoes
4 teaspoons corn-oil margarine
½ teaspoon salt
⅛ teaspoon freshly ground black pepper
12 asparagus spears, steamed crisp-tender
2 cooked large crab legs
¾ cup hollandaise sauce (see Index)

1. Cut the potatoes into halves. With a knife, slit the edges of the potato shells at 1-inch intervals, and flatten the shells and pulp to form the bases for the other ingredients.

2. Work 1 teaspoon margarine, ⅛ teaspoon salt and a pinch of pepper into each potato half with a fork.

3. Place 3 asparagus spears on each potato half. Place ½ crab leg on each potato half. Top each with 3 tablespoons of hollandaise sauce. Serve cold or at room temperature.

Makes two servings.
Each serving contains approximately 441 calories, 84 mg cholesterol, 16 gm fat, 1485 mg sodium.

Shrimp Salad in a Spud

2 baked potatoes
2 teaspoons freshly squeezed lemon juice
1 tablespoon extra-virgin olive oil
⅛ teaspoon salt
⅛ teaspoon freshly ground black pepper
¾ cup cooked shelled shrimps, coarsely chopped, OR
   ¾ cup small frozen shrimps, drained and dried
½ cup torn lettuce, in small pieces
2 tablespoons minced green onion
½ medium tomato, peeled and diced
½ small avocado, peeled and cubed
2 teaspoons finely chopped parsley

1. Cut a thin slice from the top of each potato. Remove the pulp from the potatoes, being careful not to tear the shells. Dice the potato pulp and place in a mixing bowl.

2. Combine the lemon juice, oil, salt, and pepper and mix well. Set aside.

3. Add the shrimps, lettuce, green onion, tomato, avocado, and parsley to the diced potato and mix thoroughly. Pour the lemon juice mixture over the potato mixture and toss lightly.

4. Heap the mixture into the potato shells. This is best when served immediately; however, if you wish to make them ahead of time, they can be refrigerated and served cold.

Makes two servings.
Each serving contains approximately 387 calories, 166 mg cholesterol, 13 gm fat, 356 mg sodium.

Oyster Stew Spuds

2 baked potatoes
1 tablespoon corn-oil margarine
¼ cup finely chopped onion
¼ cup finely chopped celery
1 garlic clove, finely chopped
½ cup low-fat milk
½ teaspoon salt
⅛ teaspoon white pepper
¾ cup chopped oysters
Parsley sprigs, for garnish

1. Cut a thin slice from the top of each potato. Remove the pulp from the potatoes, being careful not to tear the shells. Place the potato pulp in a mixing bowl; cover and set aside. Keep the shells warm.

2. Melt the corn-oil margarine in a saucepan. Add the onion, celery, and garlic and cook until soft.

3. While the vegetables are cooking, whip the potato pulp with a mixer and add the milk, salt, and pepper; mix well. Set aside.

4. Add the chopped oysters to the vegetables and cook until the oysters turn white. Add the whipped potato to the oyster mixture and mix thoroughly.

5. Spoon the mixture into the warm potato shells and garnish with parsley sprigs. Serve immediately.

Makes two servings.
Each serving contains approximately 335 calories, 47 mg cholesterol, 9 gm fat, 804 mg sodium.

Spicy Clam Stuffed Spud

2 baked potatoes
1 tablespoon extra-virgin olive oil
½ cup chopped onion
2 garlic cloves, minced or pressed
½ cup tomato sauce
¼ cup dry red wine
¼ cup sliced ripe olives
1 teaspoon freshly squeezed lemon juice
¼ teaspoon salt
¼ teaspoon freshly ground black pepper
2 dashes Tabasco (optional)
1 (6½-ounce) can chopped clams, drained
Parsley sprigs, for garnish (optional)

1. Cut a thin slice from the top of each potato. Remove the pulp from the potatoes, being careful not to tear the shells. Place the potato pulp in a mixing bowl and mash; cover and set aside. Keep the shells warm.

2. Heat the oil in a large skillet. Add the onion and garlic and cook over low heat until tender, about 10 minutes.

3. Combine the tomato sauce, red wine, olives, lemon juice, salt and pepper, and Tabasco, and add to the onion mixture in the skillet. Cook for an additional 5 minutes.

4. Add the mashed potatoes and mix thoroughly. Add the chopped clams and cook until the mixture is heated to serving temperature. Heap the mixture into the warm potato shells and serve immediately. Garnish with parsley sprigs if desired.

Makes two servings.
Each serving contains approximately 418 calories, 57 mg cholesterol, 11 gm fat, 918 mg sodium.

Speedy Clam Spud

2 baked potatoes
½ package (⅓ cup) dehydrated leek soup mix (Knorr or other brand)
½ cup boiling water
1 (6½-ounce) can chopped clams, drained
⅛ teaspoon freshly ground black pepper
Chopped parsley, for garnish

1. Cut a thin slice from the top of each potato. Remove the pulp from the potatoes, being careful not to tear the shells. Place the potato pulp in a mixing bowl and mash; cover and set aside. Keep the shells warm.

2. Combine the leek soup mix and water, and mix well. Add the mashed potato, chopped clams, and pepper, and heat through. Heap the mixture into the warm potato shells. Garnish with chopped parsley.

Makes two servings.
Each serving contains approximately 310 calories, 57 mg cholesterol, 2 gm fat, 255 mg sodium.

Seafood Curry with Capers Spud

2 baked potatoes
1 teaspoon canola oil
¼ cup chopped onion
1½ teaspoons curry powder
1 (6-ounce) can seafood (crab, lobster, shrimp), drained, rinsed
    under cold water, drained again thoroughly, flaked
½ cup low-fat milk
2 tablespoons capers, drained
Cayenne pepper, for garnish (optional)

1. Cut a thin slice from the top of each potato. Remove the pulp from the potatoes, being careful not to tear the shells. Place the potato pulp in a mixing bowl and mash; cover and set aside. Keep the shells warm.

2. Heat the oil in a large skillet. Cook the onion over low heat until tender, about 10 minutes. Add the curry powder and seafood to the onion in the skillet. Stir slightly.

3. Add the milk to the mashed potato and mix well. Add to the ingredients in the skillet, lightly folding and heating through. Add the capers and mix well.

4. Heap the mixture into the warm potato shells and garnish very lightly with cayenne pepper.

Makes two servings.
Each serving contains approximately 324 calories, 80 mg cholesterol, 5 gm fat, 995 mg sodium.

Seafood Stew Spud

2 baked potatoes
1 tablespoon corn-oil margarine
¼ cup finely chopped onion
¼ cup finely chopped celery
1 garlic clove, minced or pressed
½ cup low-fat milk
½ teaspoon salt
⅛ teaspoon white pepper
¾ cup chopped shrimps, crab, lobster, leftover fish, or a combination
Parsley sprigs, for garnish

1. Cut a thin slice from the top of each potato. Remove the pulp from the potatoes, being careful not to tear the shells. Place the potato pulp in a mixing bowl; cover and set aside. Keep the shells warm.

2. Melt the margarine in a saucepan. Add the onion, celery, and garlic and cook until soft, about 10 minutes.

3. While the vegetables are cooking, whip the potato pulp with a mixer and add the milk, salt, and pepper; mix well. Set aside.

4. Add the chopped seafood to the sautéed vegetables and cook until the fish is thoroughly heated. Add the whipped potato to the fish mixture, mix thoroughly, and heat through. Heap the mixture into the warm potato shells and garnish with parsley sprigs.

Makes two servings.
Each serving contains approximately 373 calories, 45 mg cholesterol, 9 gm fat, 762 mg sodium.

Gravlax Stuffed Spud

2 baked potatoes
¼ cup cider vinegar
2 teaspoons dry mustard
1 egg, lightly beaten
¼ cup nonfat milk
1 tablespoon corn-oil margarine
1 tablespoon fructose
1 cup chopped gravlax (Scandinavian Pickled Salmon [recipe follows])
Fresh dill or parsley sprigs, for garnish (optional)

1. Cut a thin slice from the top of each potato. Remove the pulp from the potatoes, being careful not to tear the shells. Crumble the pulp and set aside in a covered bowl. Set the shells aside.

2. Combine the vinegar and mustard and stir until the mustard is completely dissolved. Add the beaten egg and milk, and mix well.

3. Pour the mixture into a saucepan and slowly bring to a boil, stirring constantly with a wire whisk. Continue stirring and allow to simmer for no more than 1 minutes. Remove from the heat and put the margarine on top of the sauce. DO NOT STIR! Allow to cool to room temperature. Add the fructose and again stir with a wire whisk until thoroughly mixed.

4. Combine the potato, mustard sauce and gravlax and heap into the potato shells. Garnish with fresh dill if available, or parsley sprigs. Serve at room temperature.

Makes two servings.
Each serving contains approximately 470 calories, 170 mg cholesterol, 16 gm fat, 1360 mg sodium.

Gravlax

If you are unable to find gravlax in a delicatessen, here is a recipe.

1 teaspoon dried dill weed
1 teaspoon dill seed
2 tablespoons salt
2 teaspoons fructose
1/4 teaspoon freshly ground black pepper
2 pounds fresh salmon (a center section fillet with the skin is best)
3/4 cup red wine vinegar

1. Using a mortar and pestle, crush the dill weed and dill seed, salt, fructose, and black pepper together thoroughly. Sprinkle half of this mixture in the bottom of a glass dish just large enough to hold the salmon.

2. Place the salmon, skin side down, in the dish and rub the remaining herb mixture into the fish well, using your hands.

3. Pour the vinegar over the fish and cover tightly with plastic wrap or aluminum foil. Place a weight of at least 1 pound on top of the fish (I use a can of fruit or vegetables for this purpose).

4. Refrigerate for at least 2 days, spooning the juices over the marinating salmon as frequently as possible (at least five times a day).

Makes eight 4-ounce servings.
Each serving contains approximately 170 calories, 62 mg cholesterol, 7 gm fat, 1350 mg sodium.

Lox 'n' Spuds

Lox 'n' Spuds will replace Lox 'n' Bagels for real potato fanciers. Try it, you'll love it!

2 baked potatoes
2 tablespoons corn-oil margarine
½ cup light sour cream
½ teaspoon salt
Freshly ground black pepper
4 slices red onion
3 ounces smoked salmon (lox)
4 tablespoons light cream cheese, softened
Light sour cream, for garnish

1. Cut the potatoes into halves. With a knife slit the edges of the potato shells at 1-inch intervals, and flatten the shells and pulp to form the 4 bases (the "bagels") for the other ingredients. Using a fork, work 1½ teaspoons margarine, 2 tablespoons sour cream, ⅛ teaspoon salt, and a dash of pepper into each potato half.

2. Place a slice of red onion on each potato half. Divide the smoked salmon evenly over the 4 portions, reserving a small amount for topping.

3. Spread 1 tablespoon cream cheese over the salmon on each potato, and top each with remaining pieces of salmon and a teaspoon of sour cream.

Makes two servings.
Each serving contains approximately 460 calories, 44 mg cholesterol, 24 gm fat, 1153 mg sodium.

Sockeye Salmon Spud

2 baked potatoes
1 tablespoon corn-oil margarine
1 medium onion, finely chopped
¼ cup chicken stock (see Index)
Pinch of white pepper
¼ teaspoon salt
1 teaspoon Worcestershire sauce
1 tablespoon freshly squeezed lemon juice
1 (7¾-ounce) can sockeye salmon, drained and flaked
½ cup light sour cream
Chopped parsley, for garnish (optional)

1. Cut a thin slice from the top of each potato. Remove the pulp from the potatoes, being careful not to tear the shells. Place the potato pulp in a mixing bowl and mash; cover and set aside. Keep the shells warm.

2. Heat the margarine in a skillet. Add the onion and cook over low heat until tender, about 10 minutes. Add the chicken stock, pepper, salt, Worcestershire sauce, and lemon juice. Add the salmon and mix thoroughly.

3. Combine the potatoes and sour cream and mix well. Add to the salmon mixture; heat thoroughly. Heap into the warm potato shells and garnish with chopped parsley.

Makes two servings.
Each serving contains approximately 507 calories, 67 mg cholesterol, 21 gm fat, 969 mg sodium.

Baked Tuna in a Spud

2 baked potatoes
1 onion, chopped
2 tablespoons corn-oil margarine
½ teaspoon salt
⅛ teaspoon freshly ground black pepper
1 teaspoon basil, crushed in a mortar with a pestle
1 (6⅛-ounce) can water-packed tuna, drained and flaked
1 large tomato, diced
½ cup low-fat milk
2 tablespoons freshly grated Parmesan cheese

1. Cut a thin slice from the top of each potato. Remove the pulp from the potatoes, being careful not to tear the shells. Place the potato pulp in a mixing bowl and mash; cover and set aside. Keep the shells warm.

2. Sauté the onion in the margarine. Add the salt, pepper, basil, and tuna, and cook for 5 minutes.

3. Add the mashed potato, diced tomato and milk, and mix well. Heap the mixture into the potato shells and cover each potato with 1 tablespoon Parmesan cheese.

4. Bake at 350°F for 15 minutes.

Makes two servings.
Each serving contains approximately 473 calories, 22 mg cholesterol, 14 gm fat, 1117 mg sodium.

Chopstick Tuna Spud

2 baked potatoes
½ cup canned condensed low-salt mushroom soup
1 tablespoon peanut or sesame oil
¼ cup diagonal slices of celery or green bell pepper
¼ cup chopped onion
1 (6⅛-ounce) can water-packed tuna, drained and flaked
1 tablespoon sodium-reduced soy sauce
¼ cup dry roasted cashews
¼ cup chow mein noodles, broken in pieces

1. Cut a thin slice from the top of each potato. Remove the pulp from the potatoes, being careful not to tear the shells. Place the potato pulp in a mixing bowl. Add the soup and mix thoroughly; set aside. Keep the shells warm.

2. Heat the oil in a skillet. Add the celery or bell pepper and the onion, and cook over low heat until tender.

3. Add the tuna, soup and potato mixture, and soy sauce, and mix thoroughly. Heat through.

4. Add the cashews and toss lightly. Heap the mixture into the warm potato shells. Top with chow mein noodles. (If you are making these ahead of time, add the chow mein noodles after you have reheated the spuds in a 350° F oven for 15 minutes.)

Makes two servings.
Each serving contains approximately 469 calories, 13 mg cholesterol, 15 gm fat, 643 mg sodium.

Creamed Tuna Stuffed Spud

¼ cup chopped raw almonds
2 baked potatoes
1 tablespoon corn-oil margarine
¼ cup chopped onion
¼ cup chopped green bell pepper
1 (6⅛-ounce) can water-packed tuna, drained
3 tablespoons dry white wine
2 tablespoons chopped pimiento
2 tablespoons chopped parsley
½ teaspoon salt
½ teaspoon freshly ground black pepper
1 cup white sauce (see Index)
¼ cup nonfat milk
Pinch of paprika
Pimiento strips, for garnish (optional)

1. Toast the chopped almonds in a 350°F oven for 8 to 10 minutes, or until golden brown. Watch them carefully as they burn easily. Set aside.

2. Cut a thin slice from the top of each potato. Remove the pulp from the potatoes, being careful not to tear the shells. Place the potato pulp in a mixing bowl and mash; cover and set aside. Keep the shells warm.

3. Heat the margarine in a large skillet. Add the onion and bell pepper and cook over low heat until tender, about 10 minutes. Add the tuna, wine, pimiento, parsley, salt, and pepper and mix well. Stir in the white sauce.

4. Add the milk to the mashed potato; mix well. Add to the other ingredients in the skillet and cook to serving temperature. Add the toasted almonds within the last minute of cooking.

5. Heap the mixture into the warm potato shells and garnish with paprika and pimiento strips.

Makes two servings.
Each serving contains approximately 640 calories, 23 mg cholesterol, 29 gm fat, 1296 mg sodium.

Tuna Casserole Spud

2 baked potatoes
1 tablespoon corn-oil margarine
¼ cup chopped onion
¼ cup chopped green bell pepper
¼ cup chopped celery
½ cup canned condensed low-salt cream of mushroom soup
¼ cup nonfat milk
2 tablespoons nonfat, cholesterol-free mayonnaise dressing
1 tablespoon chopped pimiento
1 (6⅛-ounce) can water-packed tuna, drained and flaked
¼ teaspoon salt
⅛ teaspoon freshly ground black pepper
¼ cup grated 20% fat-reduced cheddar cheese
Snipped chives or green onion tops, for garnish

1. Cut a thin slice from the top of each potato. Remove the pulp from the potatoes, being careful not to tear the shells. Place the potato pulp in a mixing bowl and mash; cover and set aside. Keep the shells warm.

2. Heat the margarine in a large skillet. Add the onion, bell pepper, and celery and cook over low heat until tender, about 10 minutes.

3. Combine the soup, milk, and mashed potato and mix well. Add to the skillet ingredients; stir well. Combine the mayonnaise, pimiento, tuna, salt, and pepper and add to the potato mixture; heat through. Add the cheese and stir until the cheese has melted and blended with the other ingredients.

4. Heap the mixture into the warm potato shells. Garnish with snipped chives or green onion tops.

Makes two servings.
Each serving contains approximately 431 calories, 28 mg cholesterol, 10 gm fat, 1133 mg sodium.

Variation: CHICKEN CASSEROLE SPUD. Substitute ¾ cup chopped cooked chicken for the tuna.

Salade Niçoise Spud

2 baked potatoes
1 tomato, diced
1 (2-ounce) can flat fillets of anchovy, rinsed, dried, and
  coarsely chopped
¼ cup coarsely chopped pitted ripe olives
2 leaves of Bibb lettuce, torn into small pieces
1 leaf of romaine lettuce, torn into small pieces
½ cup Jet Fuel Dressing, tarragon variation (see Index)
2 leaves of romaine lettuce for lining potato shells
Chopped parsley, for garnish

1. Cut a thin slice from the top of each potato. Cool to room temperature and remove the pulp from the potatoes, being careful not to tear the shells. Dice the potato pulp and place in a mixing bowl. Set the shells aside.

2. Add the tomato, cucumber, anchovies, olives, and torn lettuce to the diced potatoes and mix well. Add the dressing and toss thoroughly.

3. Line the potato shells with romaine lettuce leaves and heap the salad mixture into the shells. Garnish with chopped parsley. (Salade Niçoise is best served at room temperature; however, if you are making it ahead of time, it can be refrigerated and served cold.)

Makes two servings.
Each serving contains approximately 278 calories, 24 mg cholesterol, 5 gm fat, 871 mg sodium.

Jansson's Temptation in a Spud

This is an adaption of a popular Scandinavian potato casserole. This recipe is not only delicious, but so different that in my novel, *Ambition's Woman*, I selected it for the heroine, an overnight Broadway star, to prepare for her favorite boyfriend, an up-and-coming young director, the first time she invited him for dinner.

2 baked potatoes
1 tablespoon corn-oil margarine
1 large onion, finely chopped
1 (2-ounce) can flat anchovy fillets, rinsed, dried, and finely chopped
½ cup low-fat milk
⅛ teaspoon white pepper
1 tablespoon fine bread crumbs

1.   Cut a thin slice from the top of each potato. Remove the pulp from the potatoes, being careful not to tear the shells. Place the potato pulp in a bowl and crumble; cover and set aside. Keep the shells warm.

2.   Melt the margarine in a skillet. Add the onion and cook over low heat for about 5 minutes. Add the chopped anchovies and mix thoroughly. Continue to cook for 5 more minutes, stirring frequently so that the onion does not brown.

3.   Add the milk and white pepper. Mix well. Add the crumbled potatoes and again mix well. Continue cooking until most of the liquid is absorbed.

4.   Heap the mixture into the warm potato shells and sprinkle 1½ teaspoons bread crumbs over the top of each potato. Bake in a 350°F oven for 40 minutes.

Makes two servings.
Each serving contains approximately 386 calories, 29 mg cholesterol, 10 gm fat, 680 mg sodium.

POULTRY STUFFED SPUDS

Potatoes may replace dumplings in importance as a delicious combination with chicken and turkey. Poultry stuffed spuds will certainly solve all of your problems with holiday turkey leftovers. In fact the Turkey and Cranberry Spud even gives you a perfect use for leftover cranberry sauce and is a delicious entrée served hot or cold.

If you like chicken livers, you will love Chopped Chicken Livers in a Spud. I serve the pâté variation of this recipe as an hors d'oeuvre and always get compliments.

Curried Chicken in Spuds

2 baked potatoes
1 tablespoon corn-oil margarine
½ cup chopped onion
½ cup chicken stock (see Index)
2 teaspoons curry powder
½ teaspoon salt
⅛ teaspoon ground ginger
½ cup finely chopped apple
¾ cup cooked chicken, diced without skin
¼ cup low-fat milk

1. Cut a thin slice from the top of each potato. Remove the pulp from the potatoes, being careful not to tear the shells. Place the potato pulp in a mixing bowl and mash; cover and set aside. Keep the shells warm.

2. Heat the margarine in a large skillet. Add the onion and cook over low heat until tender, about 10 minutes. Add the chicken stock, curry powder, salt, ginger, apple, and chicken, and cook for another 10 minutes.

3. Add the milk to the potato pulp and mix thoroughly. Add the potato mixture to the ingredients in the skillet and heat thoroughly. Heap the mixture into the warm potato shells and serve immediately.

Makes two servings.
Each serving contains approximately 426 calories, 75 mg cholesterol, 11 gm fat, 771 mg sodium.

Chutney and Chicken Spud

2 baked potatoes
1 tablespoon canola oil
½ cup chopped green onions, including the tops
½ cup plain nonfat yogurt
1 teaspoon curry powder
¼ cup chopped chutney
¾ cup cooked chicken, cubed without skin
¼ cup chopped dry-roasted unsalted peanuts
Chopped egg white, raisins, pineapple, or any other classic
    condiments (optional)

1. Cut the potatoes into halves. Scoop out the pulp, being careful not to tear the shells. Place the potato pulp in a mixing bowl and mash; cover and set aside. Keep the shells warm.

2. Heat the oil in a skillet. Add the chopped green onions and cook over low heat until tender, about 10 minutes.

3. Combine the yogurt, curry powder, chutney, mashed potato, chicken, and peanuts, and add to the cooked onions in the skillet. Mix well and heat to serving temperature.

4. Heap the mixture into the warm potato shells. Serve with an assortment of classic condiments if desired.

Makes two servings.
Each serving contains approximately 525 calories, 73 mg cholesterol, 20 gm fat, 120 mg sodium.

Creamed Chicken Stuffed Spud

2 tablespoons chopped raw almonds
2 baked potatoes
1 tablespoon corn-oil margarine
¼ cup chopped onion
¼ cup chopped green bell pepper
¾ cup cooked chicken, chopped without skin
3 tablespoons dry white wine
2 tablespoons chopped pimiento
2 tablespoons chopped parsley
¼ teaspoon salt
¼ teaspoon freshly ground black pepper
1 cup white sauce (see Index)
¼ cup nonfat milk
Pinch of paprika
Pimiento strips, for garnish (optional)

1. Toast the chopped almonds in a preheated 350°F oven for 8 to 10 minutes, or until golden brown. Watch them carefully as they burn easily. Set aside.

2. Cut a thin slice from the top of each potato. Remove the pulp from the potatoes, being careful not to tear the shells. Place the potato pulp in a mixing bowl and mash; cover and set aside. Keep the shells warm.

3. Heat the margarine in a large skillet. Add the onion and bell pepper and cook over low heat until tender, about 10 minutes. Add the chicken, wine, pimiento, parsley, salt, and pepper and mix well.

4. Add the milk to the mashed potato. Mix well and add to the other ingredients in the skillet. Cook to serving temperature. Add the toasted almonds within the last minute of cooking.

5. Heap the mixture into warm potato shells and garnish with paprika and pimiento strips.

Makes two servings.
Each serving contains approximately 632 calories, 82 mg cholesterol, 28 gm fat, 806 mg sodium.

Chicken Tarragon Stuffed Spud

2 tablespoons chopped walnuts
2 baked potatoes
¼ cup nonfat, cholesterol-free mayonnaise dressing
½ cup light sour cream
¼ teaspoon salt
1 teaspoon tarragon, crushed in a mortar with a pestle
¾ cup cooked chicken, chopped without skin

1. Toast the walnuts in a preheated 350°F oven for 8 to 10 minutes, or until golden brown. Watch them carefully as they burn easily. Set aside.

2. Cut a thin slice from the top of each potato. Remove the pulp from the potatoes, being careful not to tear the shells. Place the potato pulp in a bowl and mash. Keep the shells warm.

3. Add the mayonnaise, sour cream, salt, and tarragon to the mashed potatoes and mix thoroughly. Add the chicken and toasted walnuts, reserving enough of the walnuts to sprinkle over the tops for garnish.

4. Heap the mixture into the potato shells. Bake in a 350°F oven for 15 minutes. Garnish with the reserved walnuts before serving.

Makes two servings.
Each serving contains approximately 469 calories, 96 mg cholesterol, 15 gm fat, 773 mg sodium.

Chicken Surprise Stuffed Spud

2 baked potatoes
1 tablespoon corn-oil margarine
1 cup frozen French-cut green beans, defrosted
1/3 cup low-fat milk
2 tablespoons sodium-reduced soy sauce
1/2 cup light sour cream
3/4 cup cooked chicken, cubed without skin
1/2 cup water chestnuts, drained and thinly sliced
1/8 teaspoon paprika

1. Cut a thin slice from the top of each potato. Remove the pulp from the potatoes, being careful not to tear the shells. Place the potato pulp in a mixing bowl and mash; cover and set aside. Keep the shells warm.

2. Melt the margarine in a large saucepan. Add the green beans, milk, and soy sauce and heat slowly, stirring constantly. Stir in the sour cream and mashed potatoes. Add the cubed chicken and water chestnuts. Stir lightly until the mixture is heated thoroughly.

3. Heap the mixture into the warm potato shells and garnish with paprika.

Makes two servings.
Each serving contains approximately 515 calories, 99 mg cholesterol, 17 gm fat, 790 mg sodium.

Variation: HAM SURPRISE STUFFED SPUD. Substitute 3/4 cup cubed cooked lean ham for the chicken.

Chicken and Cheese Stuffed Spud

2 baked potatoes
1 tablespoon canola oil
¼ cup sliced green onions
1 teaspoon dry mustard powder
1 teaspoon grated lemon rind
½ cup grated 20% fat-reduced Monterey Jack cheese
Pinch of freshly grated nutmeg
¼ teaspoon salt
⅛ teaspoon freshly ground black pepper
½ cup nonfat milk
½ cup cooked chicken, chopped without skin
2 tablespoons chopped dry-roasted unsalted peanuts
Chopped parsley, for garnish

1. Cut a thin slice from the top of each potato. Remove the pulp from the potatoes, being careful not to tear the shells. Place the potato pulp in a mixing bowl and mash; cover and set aside. Keep the shells warm.

2. Heat the oil in a skillet. Add the green onions and cook over low heat until tender, about 10 minutes. While the onions are cooking, combine the mustard, lemon rind, grated cheese, nutmeg, salt, and pepper and set aside.

3. Heat the milk and add it to the mashed potatoes; mix thoroughly. Add potato mixture and cheese mixture to the onions in the skillet, stirring lightly until the cheese is melted and the mixture is thoroughly heated.

4. Add the chicken and peanuts and stir until chicken is heated through. Heap the mixture into the warm potato shells and garnish with parsley.

Makes two servings.
Each serving contains approximately 490 calories, 69 mg cholesterol, 20 gm fat, 540 mg sodium.

Chicken Florentine Stuffed Spud

2 baked potatoes
¾ cup cooked spinach, drained and chopped
½ cup cooked chicken, chopped without skin
½ cup white sauce (see Index)
½ cup grated part-skim mozzarella cheese
⅛ teaspoon freshly grated nutmeg
⅛ teaspoon white pepper
1 tablespoon freshly grated Parmesan cheese

1. Cut a thin slice from the top of each potato. Remove the pulp from the potatoes, being careful not to tear the shells. Place the potato pulp in a bowl and mash. Keep the shells warm.

2. Add the spinach, chicken, white sauce, mozzarella cheese, nutmeg, and white pepper to the mashed potatoes and mix thoroughly.

3. Heap the mixture into the potato shells. Sprinkle the Parmesan cheese evenly over the tops. Bake in a 350°F oven for 15 minutes.

Makes two servings.
Each serving contains approximately 458 calories, 71 mg cholesterol, 15 gm fat, 447 mg sodium.

Variation: FISH FLORENTINE STUFFED SPUD. Substitute ½ cup chopped cooked white fish, for the chicken.

Chopped Chicken Livers in a Spud

2 baked potatoes
1 tablespoon corn-oil margarine
½ pound fresh chicken livers
2 tablespoons brandy
½ cup chicken stock (see Index)
¼ teaspoon salt
¼ teaspoon freshly ground black pepper
Chopped parsley, for garnish

1. Cut a thin slice from the top of each potato. Remove the pulp from the potatoes, being careful not to tear the shells. Place the potato pulp in a mixing bowl and mash; cover and set aside. Keep the shells warm.

2. Heat the margarine in a skillet. Add the chicken livers and cook over medium-low heat until tender. Chop the chicken livers coarsely and add the brandy, chicken stock, salt, and pepper; mix thoroughly.

3. Add the liver mixture to the mashed potatoes and mix well. Heat the mixture thoroughly. Heap into the warm potato shells and garnish with chopped parsley.

Makes two servings.
Each serving contains approximately 375 calories, 537 mg cholesterol, 11 gm fat, 436 mg sodium.

Variation: PÂTÉ IN A SPUD. Instead of chopping the chicken livers, place them in a blender container with the brandy, chicken stock, salt, and pepper. Blend until smooth before adding to the mashed potatoes; mix well.

Stuffed Spud
Marco Polo

2 baked potatoes
¾ cup white sauce (see Index)
¼ cup cooked turkey, diced without skin
¼ cup cooked lean ham, diced
⅓ cup cooked broccoli, chopped

1. Cut a thin slice from the top of each potato. Remove the pulp from the potatoes, being careful not to tear the shells. Keep the shells warm.

2. Mash the potato pulp with ½ cup of the white sauce, reserving the remaining ¼ cup to put on the top. Add the cooked turkey, ham, and broccoli, and mix gently.

3. Heap into the warm potato shells, spoon 2 tablespoons white sauce over each potato and put under the broiler until lightly browned.

Makes two servings.
Each serving contains approximately 402 calories, 35 mg cholesterol, 13 gm fat, 612 mg sodium.

Turkey and Cranberry Spud

2 baked potatoes
½ cup white sauce (see Index)
½ cup canned whole-berry cranberry sauce
¾ cup cooked turkey, chopped without skin
Cranberries (from the can), for garnish

1. Cut a thin slice from the top of each potato. Remove the pulp from the potatoes, being careful not to tear the shells. Place the potato pulp in a mixing bowl and mash; cover and set aside. Keep the shells warm.

2. Add the white sauce, cranberry sauce, and chopped turkey to the potato; mix well. Heap the mixture into the warm potato shells and heat in a 350°F oven for 15 minutes. Garnish with whole cranberries from the can before serving.

Makes two servings.
Each serving contains approximately 505 calories, 63 mg cholesterol, 10 gm fat, 257 mg sodium.

Turkey Vegetable Spud

2 baked potatoes
1 tablespoon canola oil
¼ cup sliced green onions
¼ cup shredded carrot
¼ cup chopped mushrooms
½ cup cooked turkey, cubed without skin
½ cup light sour cream
¼ cup nonfat milk
½ cup grated 20% fat-reduced cheddar cheese
½ cup steamed broccoli, cut into small pieces
¼ teaspoon salt
⅛ teaspoon pepper

1. Cut a thin slice from the top of each potato. Remove the pulp from the potatoes, being careful not to tear the shells. Place the potato pulp in a mixing bowl and mash; cover and set aside. Keep the shells warm.

2. Heat the oil in a large skillet. Add the green onion slices and cook over low heat until tender, about 10 minutes. Add the carrot, mushrooms, and turkey and cook for another 10 minutes.

3. Add the sour cream and milk to the mashed potato and mix thoroughly. Add to the other ingredients in the skillet and mix well until heated through. Add ¼ cup of the grated cheese and mix thoroughly as it melts.

4. Add the broccoli, salt, and pepper; mix well and heat through. Heap the mixture into the warm potato shells and sprinkle the remaining cheese over the tops. Place under the broiler until the cheese is lightly browned.

Makes two servings.
Each serving contains approximately 528 calories, 87 mg cholesterol, 23 gm fat, 492 mg sodium.

Chicken or Turkey Hash in a Spud

2 baked potatoes
1 tablespoon canola oil
¼ cup chopped onion
2 tablespoons chopped parsley
¾ cup cooked chicken or turkey, chopped without skin
1 tablespoon sodium-reduced soy sauce
⅓ cup nonfat milk
¼ teaspoon thyme, crushed in a mortar with a pestle
Chopped parsley, for garnish

1. Cut a thin slice from the top of each potato. Remove the pulp from the potatoes, being careful not to tear the shells. Place the potato pulp in a mixing bowl and mash; cover and set aside. Keep the shells warm.

2. Heat the oil in a large skillet. Add the onion and parsley, and cook over low heat until tender, about 10 minutes. Add the chopped cooked chicken or turkey and the soy sauce, and cook until the mixture is thoroughly heated.

3. While the mixture is heating, add the milk to the mashed potato and mix well. Add the thyme and mix well. Add the potato mixture to the poultry mixture and continue to cook until the mixture is heated through, stirring well.

4. Heap the mixture into the warm potato shells and garnish with chopped parsley.

Makes two servings.
Each serving contains approximately 395 calories, 59 mg cholesterol, 10 gm fat, 387 mg sodium.

White Chili Bowl Spud

2 baked potatoes
1 tablespoon canola oil
1 medium onion, chopped
1 garlic clove, chopped
2 canned green Ortega chiles, seeded and chopped
½ teaspoon cumin seed
½ teaspoon oregano, crushed in a mortar with a pestle
¼ teaspoon ground coriander
¼ teaspoon salt
Pinch of cayenne pepper
½ cup cooked chicken or turkey, chopped without skin
½ cup cooked white beans
Chopped fresh cilantro or green onion tops, for garnish

1. Cut a thin slice from the top of each potato. Remove the pulp from the potatoes, being careful not to tear the shells. Place the potato pulp in a bowl and crumble; cover and set aside. Keep the shells warm.

2. Heat the oil in a skillet. Cook the onion and garlic over low heat until onion is clear and tender. Add the chopped chiles and all seasonings, and mix well. Add the crumbled potatoes; mix well. Cook for another 5 minutes.

3. Add the chopped chicken or turkey and the beans and heat thoroughly. Heap into the warm potato shells and garnish with fresh cilantro or green onion tops.

Makes two servings.
Each serving contains approximately 424 calories, 39 mg cholesterol, 10 gm fat, 347 mg sodium.

Eclectic Salad in Potato Pockets

If you like pita pockets, you will most certainly like potato pockets. Try this recipe and then use your own imagination to make potato pockets with whatever leftover bits and pieces you may have in the refrigerator.

2 baked potatoes
½ cup cooked chicken or turkey, cubed without skin
¼ cup alfalfa sprouts or bean sprouts
½ cup low-fat cottage cheese
¼ cup chopped red bell pepper
¼ cup chopped green bell pepper
¼ cup chopped radishes
2 slices Canadian bacon, cooked and diced
2 tablespoons toasted sunflower seeds
¼ teaspoon freshly squeezed lemon juice
2 lettuce leaves
4 tomato slices

1. Slit the tops of the baked potatoes; leaving approximately ⅛-inch of potato pulp in the shells, remove the rest, being careful not to tear the shells. Place the potato pulp in the refrigerator for use at another meal (see Helpful Hints). Flatten the shells to form "pockets."

2. Combine the chicken, sprouts, cottage cheese, red and green bell peppers, radishes, bacon, toasted sunflower seeds, and lemon juice, and mix thoroughly. Chill.

3. Line the potato pockets with the lettuce leaves. Spoon the mixture into the pockets, interspersed with tomato slices.

Makes two servings.
Each serving contains approximately 345 calories, 56 mg cholesterol, 9 gm fat, 683 mg sodium.

MEAT STUFFED SPUDS

Meat and potatoes have long been considered the staple American diet by many people. Meat stuffed spuds help to make this concept easier, less expensive, and more fun. Whether you are planning a backyard picnic with Tex-Mex Chili Spuds or Sloppy Joe Spuds, a Sunday brunch with Spuds Benedict or Green Eggs and Ham in Spuds, or a St. Patrick's Day party with either Corned Beef and Cabbage Spuds or Irish Tacos, you will delight your guests and save yourself time and money.

Beef Hash in a Spud

2 baked potatoes
1 tablespoon canola oil
¼ cup chopped onion
2 tablespoons chopped parsley
1 cup coarsely ground lean beef
1 tablespoon Worcestershire sauce
⅓ cup nonfat milk
¼ teaspoon salt
⅛ teaspoon freshly ground black pepper
Chopped parsley, for garnish

1. Cut a thin slice from the top of each potato. Remove the pulp from the potatoes, being careful not to tear the shells. Place the potato pulp in a mixing bowl and mash; cover and set aside. Keep the shells warm.

2. Heat the oil in a skillet. Add the onion and parsley and cook over low heat until tender, about 10 minutes. Add the ground beef and Worcestershire sauce, and cook until the beef is just barely pink.

3. While the beef is cooking, stir the milk into the mashed potato. Add the salt and pepper and mix well.

4. Add the potato mixture to the beef mixture and continue to cook until thoroughly heated, mixing well. Heap the mixture into the warm potato shells and garnish with chopped parsley.

Makes two servings.
Each serving contains approximately 433 calories, 87 mg cholesterol, 15 gm fat, 477 mg sodium.

New England Stuffed Spud

2 baked potatoes
¾ cup beef stock (see Index)
1 bay leaf
¼ cup chopped onion
¼ cup finely chopped carrot
¼ cup finely chopped celery
¼ teaspoon salt
¼ teaspoon freshly ground black pepper
½ cup shredded cabbage
¾ cup chopped cooked lean beef brisket, or other leftover
  cooked lean beef
Snipped chives or green onion tops, for garnish

1. Cut a thin slice from the top of each potato. Cool potatoes to room temperature. Remove the pulp from the potatoes, being careful not to tear the shells. Dice the potato pulp and set aside.

2. Heat the beef stock in a saucepan. Add the bay leaf, onion, carrot, celery, salt, and pepper, and cook until the carrot is tender, about 10 minutes. Discard the bay leaf.

3. Add the cabbage and diced potato, and mix thoroughly. Add the chopped beef and mix thoroughly. Heap the mixture into the potato shells and bake in a 350°F oven for 15 minutes. Garnish with snipped chives or green onion tops.

Makes two servings.
Each serving contains approximately 447 calories, 86 mg cholesterol, 16 gm fat, 435 mg sodium.

Sloppy Joe Spud

2 baked potatoes
1 tablespoon canola oil
¼ cup chopped green onions
1 cup cooked lean ground round
3 tablespoons Sloppy Joe seasoning mix
1 cup tomato sauce
Dash of Tabasco (optional)
Snipped chives or green onion tops, for garnish (optional)

1. Cut a thin slice from the top of each potato. Remove the pulp from the potatoes, being careful not to tear the shells. Place the potato pulp in a mixing bowl and mash; cover and set aside. Keep the shells warm.

2. Heat the oil in a saucepan. Add the green onions, ground beef, seasoning mix, tomato sauce, and Tabasco; mix well. Cook over low heat for 10 minutes, stirring regularly. Add the mashed potatoes and mix thoroughly until the potatoes are heated through.

3. Heap the mixture into the warm potato shells and garnish with snipped chives or green onion tops.

Makes two servings.
Each serving contains approximately 545 calories, 95 mg cholesterol, 16 gm fat, 2000 mg sodium.

Reuben Spud

2 baked potatoes
2 tablespoons nonfat, cholesterol-free mayonnaise dressing
¼ cup nonfat milk
1 tablespoon prepared horseradish
¾ cup sauerkraut, drained
¼ cup chopped green onions
⅛ teaspoon salt
⅛ teaspoon freshly ground black pepper
¾ cup small pieces of cooked corned beef
½ cup grated 20% fat-reduced Swiss or Gruyère cheese

1. Cut a thin slice from the top of each potato. Remove the pulp from the potatoes, being careful not to tear the shells. Place the potato pulp in a mixing bowl and mash; cover and set aside. Keep the shells warm.

2. Combine the mashed potato, mayonnaise and milk in a saucepan. Add the horseradish, sauerkraut, green onions, salt, pepper, corn beef, and half of the cheese; mix thoroughly. Cook over low heat until the mixture is thoroughly heated.

3. Heap the mixture into the warm potato shells and sprinkle tops with the remaining grated cheese. Heat in a 350°F oven or under a broiler until the cheese has melted.

Makes two servings.
Each serving contains approximately 485 calories, 99 mg cholesterol, 20 gm fat, 1816 mg sodium.

Corned Beef and Cabbage Spud

2 baked potatoes
1 tablespoon canola oil
¼ cup chopped onion
1 garlic clove, minced or pressed
3 tablespoons dry red wine
¾ cup chopped corned beef
1 tablespoon spicy brown mustard
1 cup shredded cabbage, cooked crisp tender
¼ cup nonfat milk
¼ teaspoon freshly ground black pepper
Snipped chives or green onion tops, for garnish

1. Cut a thin slice from the top of each potato. Remove the pulp from the potatoes, being careful not to tear the shells. Place the potato pulp in a mixing bowl and mash; cover and set aside. Keep the shells warm.

2. Heat the oil in a skillet. Add the onion and garlic, and cook over low heat until tender, about 10 minutes. Add the red wine, corned beef, and mustard, stirring well.

3. Add the cabbage, milk, salt, and pepper to the mashed potatoes and mix well. Add the potato mixture to the skillet, stirring well until heated thoroughly.

4. Heap the mixture into the warm potato shells and garnish with snipped chives or green onion tops.

Makes two servings.
Each serving contains approximately 486 calories, 84 mg cholesterol, 24 gm fat, 1398 mg sodium.

Tex-Mex Chili Spud

2 baked potatoes
1 tablespoon corn oil
¼ cup chopped green bell pepper
¼ cup chopped onion
1 garlic clove, minced or pressed
¼ cup chopped green chile peppers (2 medium)
¾ cup chile con carne
½ cup fresh tomatoes, crushed
½ teaspoon chili powder
¼ teaspoon salt
¼ teaspoon freshly ground black pepper
Chopped onion, for garnish

1. Cut a thin slice from the top of each potato. Remove the pulp from the potatoes, being careful not to tear the shells. Place the potato pulp in a mixing bowl and mash; cover and set aside. Keep the shells warm.

2. Heat the oil in a skillet. Add the bell pepper, onion, and garlic and cook over low heat until tender. Stir in the chile peppers, chile con carne, tomatoes, and chili powder. Heat thoroughly, stirring constantly.

3. Add the mashed potatoes, salt, and pepper. Stir well and heat through. Heap the mixture into the warm potato shells and garnish with chopped onion.

Makes two servings.
Each serving contains approximately 348 calories, 12 mg cholesterol, 11 gm fat, 745 mg sodium.

Variation: Top each potato with 2 tablespoons of grated sharp cheddar cheese in place of the chopped onion garnish, and place under the broiler or in the oven until the cheese has melted.

Potato Lasagna

2 baked potatoes
1 tablespoon extra-virgin olive oil
1 medium onion, finely chopped
1 clove garlic, minced or pressed
½ cup (4-ounces) lean ground round
¼ cup dry red wine
¼ cup tomato sauce
1 small tomato, peeled and chopped, OR
    ½ cup chopped canned tomato
¼ teaspoon dried basil, crushed in a mortar with a pestle
¼ teaspoon oregano, crushed in a mortar with a pestle
½ teaspoon salt
⅛ teaspoon freshly ground black pepper
½ cup grated part-skim mozzarella cheese
¼ cup sliced ripe olives
Tabasco (optional)
Chopped parsley, for garnish

1. Cut a thin slice from the top of each potato. Remove the pulp from the potatoes, being careful not to tear the shells. Place the potato pulp in a mixing bowl and mash; cover and set aside. Keep the shells warm.

2. Heat the oil in a skillet. Add the onion and garlic and cook over low heat until tender, about 10 minutes. Add the ground round, red wine, tomato sauce, tomato, basil, oregano, salt, and pepper, and cook until the meat is pink, stirring frequently.

3. Add the mashed potato pulp, mix well, and heat thoroughly. Add the cheese and olives, and Tabasco if you use it, and stir until the cheese is melted. Heap the mixture into the warm potato shells and garnish with chopped parsley.

Makes two servings.
Each serving contains approximately 469 calories, 51 mg cholesterol, 17 gm fat, 1094 mg sodium.

Variation: VEGETARIAN POTATO LASAGNA. Substitute ½ cup tempeh for the ground round.

Irish Taco

Serve this international approach to sandwich-making with extra taco sauce and chopped fresh cilantro.

2 baked potatoes
¾ cup hot cooked lean ground beef
½ cup taco sauce
½ cup 20% fat-reduced grated cheddar cheese
1 cup shredded lettuce
½ cup diced tomatoes
¼ cup chopped fresh cilantro (optional)

1. Split the tops of the potatoes. Scoop the pulp from the potatoes, one at a time, and place the pulp from one of the potatoes in a plastic bag in the freezer to use at another time. Mash remaining potato pulp in a mixing bowl. Flatten the 2 potato shells to form "taco shells," and keep warm.

2. Add the cooked ground beef to the mashed potato and mix well. Add the taco sauce and cheese, and mix thoroughly. Place the mixture into the potato shells. Top with shredded lettuce and diced tomato.

Makes two servings.
Each serving contains approximately 485 calories, 94 mg cholesterol, 14 gm fat, 426 mg sodium.

Dried Beef in a Spud

2 baked potatoes
1/3 cup dried beef, torn into small pieces
2/3 cup white sauce (see Index)
1 tablespoon prepared horseradish (optional)
Pinch of black pepper (optional)
Chopped parsley, for garnish

1. Cut a thin slice from the top of each potato. Remove the pulp from the potatoes, being careful not to tear the shells. Place the potato pulp in a mixing bowl and mash; cover and set aside. Keep the shells warm.

2. Combine the dried beef and white sauce in a saucepan and cook over low heat, stirring constantly, until the mixture starts to boil. Add the mashed potato, horseradish, and black pepper, and continue to stir until the mixture is thoroughly heated.

3. Heap the mixture into the warm potato shells. Garnish with chopped parsley.

Makes two servings.
Each serving contains approximately 364 calories, 23 mg cholesterol, 11 gm fat, 1632 mg sodium.

Steak Tartare Stuffed Spud

2 baked potatoes
1 tablespoon freshly squeezed lemon juice
½ teaspoon salt
⅛ teaspoon freshly ground black pepper
1 tablespoon Worcestershire sauce
1 drop of Tabasco
3 teaspoons prepared Dijon-style mustard
½ pound freshly ground lean beef sirloin
1 tablespoon capers
2 tablespoons minced onion
2 tablespoons minced parsley
½ cup light sour cream
1 tomato, peeled and finely diced
2 tablespoons finely diced green bell pepper

1. Cool the potatoes to room temperature. Cut into halves and remove the potato pulp; crumble and set aside. Set the shells aside.

2. Combine the lemon juice and salt, and stir until the salt is completely dissolved. Add the pepper, Worcestershire sauce, Tabasco, and 1 teaspoon of the mustard; mix thoroughly.

3. Put the meat in a mixing bowl and stir in the lemon juice mixture well. Add the capers, onion, and parsley and mix well. Add the crumbled potato, combine thoroughly, and heap into the 4 potato-shell halves.

4. Combine the sour cream and remaining 2 teaspoons mustard. Frost the tops of the Steak Tartare Stuffed Spuds with the mustard and sour cream mixture, as if frosting cakes. Sprinkle the tops with the chopped tomato and chopped green pepper. Refrigerate until cold before serving.

Makes two servings.
Each serving contains approximately 582 calories, 103 mg cholesterol, 32 gm fat, 1199 mg sodium.

Liver and Onion Stuffed Spud

2 baked potatoes
½ pound calf's liver
1 tablespoon corn-oil margarine
1 small onion, chopped
½ teaspoon salt
¼ teaspoon freshly ground black pepper
Chopped parsley, for garnish

1. Cut each potato into halves. Remove the pulp from each half, being careful not to tear the shells. Place the potato pulp in a mixing bowl and mash; cover and set aside. Keep the shells warm.

2. Wash the liver and pat it dry. Cut into ½-inch cubes and set aside.

3. Heat the margarine in a skillet. Add the onion and cook over low heat for about 15 minutes, or until very soft and nicely browned. Add the mashed potato, salt, and pepper, and cook for 5 more minutes.

4. Remove the potato and onion mixture from the pan and set aside. DO NOT WASH THE PAN! Add the cubed liver to the pan and cook for about 3 minutes. The liver should be slightly pink inside. Overcooking makes it tough and strong-tasting.

5. Combine the liver and potato mixture, and mix well. Heat thoroughly. Heap into the warm potato shells. Garnish with parsley.

Makes two servings.
Each serving contains approximately 475 calories, 373 mg cholesterol, 17 gm fat, 771 mg sodium.

German Pork and Cabbage Spud

2 baked potatoes
1 tablespoon canola oil
¼ cup chopped green onions
¾ cup chopped cooked lean pork roast
½ cup light sour cream
¾ cup sweet-and-sour red cabbage (available in jars)
¼ teaspoon salt
⅛ teaspoon freshly ground black pepper
½ cup unsweetened applesauce
Parsley sprigs, for garnish

1. Cut a thin slice from the top of each potato. Remove the pulp from the potatoes, being careful not to tear the shells. Place the potato pulp in a mixing bowl and mash; cover and set aside. Keep the shells warm.

2. Heat the oil in a skillet. Add the chopped green onions and cook over low heat until tender but not brown. Add the chopped pork, sour cream, mashed potatoes, red cabbage, salt, and pepper, and mix thoroughly. Cook until the mixture is heated through.

3. Heap the mixture into the warm potato shells. Spoon ¼ cup applesauce over each spud. Garnish with parsley sprigs and serve immediately.

Makes two servings.
Each serving contains approximately 590 calories, 106 mg cholesterol, 27 gm fat, 401 mg sodium.

Irish Lamb Stew Stuffed Spuds

2 baked potatoes
½ cup beef stock (see Index)
1 bay leaf
4 little boiling onions, peeled
3 tablespoons diced carrot
1 tablespoon finely diced celery
¼ teaspoon salt
⅛ teaspoon freshly ground black pepper
⅓ cup shredded cabbage
¼ cup frozen peas, thawed
¼ cup diced cooked lamb

1. Cut a thin slice from the top of each potato. Remove the pulp, being careful not to tear the shells. Dice the potato pulp, cover, and set aside. Keep the shells warm.

2. Heat the beef stock in a saucepan over medium-high heat. Add the bay leaf, onions, carrot, celery, salt, and pepper, and cook until the carrots are tender, about 10 minutes. Discard bay leaf and add cabbage, peas, reserved potato pulp, and diced lamb. Heat thoroughly and pile into the prepared potato shells.

Makes two servings.
Each serving contains approximately 270 calories, 28 mg cholesterol, 3 gm fat, 383 mg sodium.

Ham Quiche Spud

2 baked potatoes
1 tablespoon corn-oil margarine
¼ cup chopped onion
½ cup light sour cream
1 egg and 2 egg whites, lightly beaten
⅛ teaspoon salt
⅛ teaspoon freshly ground black pepper
¾ cup ¼-inch cubes 20% fat-reduced Swiss cheese
½ cup chopped cooked lean ham
Chopped parsley, for garnish

1. Cut a thin slice from the top of each potato. Remove the pulp from the potatoes, being careful not to tear the shells. Place the potato pulp in a mixing bowl and mash; cover and set aside. Set the shells aside.

2. Heat the margarine in a skillet. Add the onion and cook over low heat until tender, about 10 minutes. Add the sour cream, lightly beaten eggs, and the salt and pepper, stirring constantly. Add mashed potatoes and mix well. Add cubed cheese and chopped ham and mix lightly.

3. Heap the mixture into the potato shells. Bake at 350° F for 45 minutes. Garnish with chopped parsley just before serving.

Makes two servings.
Each serving contains approximately 526 calories, 169 mg cholesterol, 23 gm fat, 1027 mg sodium.

Variations: BEEF QUICHE SPUD. Substitute ½ cup chopped cooked beef for the ham, and use ¾ cup cubed sharp cheddar cheese in place of the Swiss cheese.
BACON QUICHE SPUD. Substitute 2 slices Canadian bacon, cooked and diced, for the ham. Use Swiss cheese.

Green Eggs and Ham in Spuds

This recipe was inspired by the Dr. Seuss classic, *Green Eggs and Ham*; these potatoes serve as a perfect entrée for a children's birthday party or for more adventuresome adults.

2 baked potatoes
2 tablespoons extra-virgin olive oil
1 egg and 2 egg whites
2 tablespoons nonfat milk
2 tablespoons chopped parsley
2 tablespoons snipped chives or green onion tops
⅛ teaspoon tarragon
⅛ teaspoon salt
Pinch of white pepper
¼ cup chopped cooked lean ham
2 parsley sprigs, for garnish

1. Cut a thin slice from the top of each potato. Remove the pulp carefully, leaving ¼-inch of potato to line the shells. Place the potato pulp in a mixing bowl and mash; cover and set aside.

2. Brush the insides of the potato shells with some of the oil. Place on a cookie sheet in a preheated 400°F oven and cook until browned, approximately 30 minutes.

3. Combine the egg and egg whites in a mixing bowl and beat them with a fork or wire whisk until frothy. Put the milk, chopped parsley, 1 tablespoon chives, tarragon, salt, and pepper in a blender container and blend until smooth. Pour the green mixture into the eggs and mix thoroughly.

4. Pour the remaining oil into a large skillet and heat well before adding the egg mixture. Add the eggs and reduce the heat; stir constantly until eggs are almost set. Then add the chopped ham and the potato and cook until the eggs are of a desired consistency. Be careful not to overcook or the eggs will become dry. Remove the eggs from the heat and spoon them into the toasted potato shells.

5. Sprinkle the tops with remaining snipped chives and garnish each serving with a parsley sprig.

Makes two servings.

Each serving contains approximately 393 calories, 115 mg cholesterol, 18 gm fat, 570 mg sodium.

Peas and Ham Spud

2 baked potatoes
1 package dehydrated leek soup mix (Knorr's)
¾ cup boiling water
½ cup frozen peas
¾ cup chopped cooked lean ham
⅛ teaspoon salt
⅛ teaspoon freshly ground black pepper
Chopped parsley sprigs, for garnish

1. Cut a thin slice from the top of each potato. Remove the pulp from the potatoes, being careful not to tear the shells. Place the potato pulp in a mixing bowl and mash; cover and set aside. Keep the shells warm.

2. Combine the soup mix and boiling water in a saucepan. Add the peas and cook for 5 minutes, stirring constantly. Add the mashed potatoes, heat through, and stir well. Add the ham, salt, and pepper and mix lightly.

3. Heap into the warm potato shells. Garnish with chopped parsley and serve immediately.

Makes two servings.
Each serving contains approximately 350 calories, 27 mg cholesterol, 5 gm fat, 1614 mg sodium.

Ham Souffle in Spuds

2 baked potatoes
3 tablespoons corn-oil margarine
6 tablespoons low-fat milk
¼ teaspoon salt
1½ tablespoons unbleached all-purpose flour
1 teaspoon prepared mustard
1 egg yolk, lightly beaten
¾ cup finely chopped cooked lean ham
2 egg whites

1. Cut a thin slice from the top of each potato. Remove the pulp from the potatoes, being careful not to tear the shells. Keep the shells warm.

2. Combine the potato pulp, 1 tablespoon margarine, 2 tablespoons milk, and the salt in a bowl, and whip. Cover and set aside.

3. Melt remaining margarine in a saucepan over medium heat. Add the flour, remaining milk, and the mustard and cook, stirring constantly, until thickened. Remove from heat. Add the beaten egg yolk and mix thoroughly. Stir in the ham.

4. Using the electric mixer, beat the egg whites until soft peaks form. Fold into the ham mixture. Fold the ham into the potato mixture and combine well. Heap the mixture into the potato shells and bake in a 375°F oven for 25 minutes.

Makes two servings.
Each serving contains approximately 534 calories, 136 mg cholesterol, 25 gm fat, 1587 mg sodium.

Deviled Ham Stuffed Spud

These are good served hot, warm, or cold. They make excellent picnic or brown bag lunches and are also wonderful for a cool supper on a hot night.

2 baked potatoes
1 (4½-ounce) can deviled ham
¼ cup nonfat, cholesterol-free mayonnaise dressing
¼ cup sweet pickle relish

1. Cut a thin slice from the top of each potato. Remove the pulp from the potatoes, being careful not to tear the shells. Place the potato pulp in a mixing bowl and mash. Set the shells aside.

2. Add the deviled ham to the potatoes and mash thoroughly. Add the mayonnaise and pickle relish; stir until well-mixed. Heap into the potato shells.

Makes two servings.
Each serving contains approximately 455 calories, 40 mg cholesterol, 20 gm fat, 1425 mg sodium.

Alpenspitz Stuffed Spud with Mushroom Sauce

My inspiration for this recipe came from Dagmar and Steven Brezzo's presentation of Alpenspitz' Potatoes with Mushrooms at the Celebrities Cook for Cancer Benefit in San Diego. The only difference is that their dish was not stuffed in a spud!

2 baked potatoes
3 tablespoons corn-oil margarine
1 egg yolk, lightly beaten
1/4 teaspoon salt
1/8 teaspoon freshly grated nutmeg
1 teaspoon dill weed, crushed in a mortar with a pestle
1 tablespoon minced onion
2 slices Canadian bacon, cooked and diced
3/4 cup grated 20% fat-reduced sharp cheddar cheese
2 egg whites
Mushroom Sauce:
    4 tablespoons corn-oil margarine
    1 shallot, finely chopped
    2 cups sliced fresh mushrooms
    1/2 teaspoon ground coriander
    1/8 teaspoon freshly grated nutmeg
    1 tablespoon sherry

1. Cut a thin slice from the top of each potato. Remove the pulp from the potatoes, being careful not to tear the shells. Place the potato pulp and 3 tablespoons margarine in a mixing bowl and mash. Keep the shells warm.

2. Combine the beaten egg yolk, salt, 1/8 teaspoon nutmeg, dill weed, and onion. Mix well and add the potato. Add diced bacon and grated cheese, and again mix well. Heap the mixture into the warm potato shells and bake in a 350°F oven for 30 minutes.

3. Whip the egg whites until stiff but not dry and spread over the tops of the baked potatoes. Return to the 350°F oven until the meringue is lightly browned.

4. While the potatoes are heating, make the sauce. Melt the 4 tablespoons margarine and sauté the shallot until lightly browned. Add the sliced mushrooms, coriander, nutmeg, and sherry, and sauté until the mushrooms are tender. Serve the sauce with the stuffed spud.

Makes two servings.
Each serving contains approximately 787 calories, 157 mg cholesterol, 56 gm fat, 1392 mg sodium.

Spuds Benedict

This recipe requires that several items be cooking at once, so organize your time accordingly.

2 baked potatoes
8 teaspoons corn-oil margarine
¼ teaspoon salt, approximately
4 slices Canadian bacon, cooked
4 egg whites, poached
½ cup hollandaise sauce (see Index), warm
Truffle or ripe olive slices, for garnish

1. Cut the potatoes into halves. With a knife slit the edges of the potato shells at 1-inch intervals, and flatten the shells and pulp to form the 4 bases (the "muffins") for the other ingredients. Work 2 teaspoons margarine and a pinch of salt into each potato half. Keep warm.

2. Place 1 slice of bacon on each potato half, top with a poached egg, and then some warm hollandaise sauce. Garnish with slices of truffle or ripe olive.

Makes two servings.
Each serving contains approximately 480 calories, 64 mg cholesterol, 25 gm fat, 1481 mg sodium.

Southern Turnip Stuffed Spud

2 baked potatoes
4 slices Canadian bacon
1 medium onion, chopped
1 cup mashed cooked turnip
1/4 teaspoon salt
1/4 teaspoon freshly ground black pepper
Chopped parsley, for garnish (optional)

1. Cut a thin slice from the top of each potato. Remove the pulp from the potatoes, being careful not to tear the shells. Place the potato pulp in a mixing bowl and mash; cover and set aside. Keep the shells warm.

2. Cook the bacon until lightly browned and remove from the skillet. Add the chopped onion to the skillet and cook, covered, over low heat until tender, about 10 minutes. Stir occasionally and add a little water or stock, if necessary, to prevent scorching.

3. Dice the bacon and add to the mashed potato. Add the turnip, salt, and pepper and mix well. Add to the onion in the skillet and heat thoroughly. Heap into the warm potato shells. Garnish with parsley if desired.

Makes two servings.
Each serving contains approximately 318 calories, 28 mg cholesterol, 5 gm fat, 1146 mg sodium.

Hot German Potato Salad

2 baked potatoes
4 slices Canadian bacon
2 teaspoons canola oil
¼ cup chopped green onions
¼ cup chopped green bell pepper
¼ teaspoon salt
⅛ teaspoon freshly ground black pepper
2 tablespoons cider vinegar
2 teaspoons fructose
Chopped parsley, for garnish

1. Cut a thin slice from the top of each potato. Remove the pulp from the potatoes, being careful not to tear the shells. Place the potato pulp in a mixing bowl and crumble; cover and set aside. Keep the shells warm.

2. Cook the bacon in a skillet until lightly browned. Dice and set aside. Using the same skillet, combine the oil, green onions, and bell pepper. Cook over low heat until tender, about 10 minutes. Add the vinegar, fructose, and crumbled potato and heat thoroughly, stirring lightly to keep from "mashing" the potatoes.

3. Heap the mixture into the warm potato shells and garnish with chopped parsley. This can also be served cold.

Makes two servings.
Each serving contains approximately 328 calories, 28 mg cholesterol, 9 gm fat, 1105 mg sodium.

BLT Stuffed Spud

(Bacon, Lettuce and Tomato)

2 baked potatoes
¼ cup nonfat, cholesterol-free mayonnaise dressing
4 slices Canadian bacon, cooked and diced
1 large tomato, diced
1 cup finely chopped lettuce

1. Cut a thin slice from the top of each potato. Remove the pulp from the potatoes, being careful not to tear the shells. Crumble the potato pulp.

2. Combine the potato with the mayonnaise. Add the diced bacon, tomato, and lettuce. Toss thoroughly. Stuff back into the potato shells.

Makes two servings.
Each serving contains approximately 294 calories, 28 mg cholesterol, 4 gm fat, 1193 mg sodium.

Variation: VEGETARIAN BLT STUFFED SPUD. Substitute 4 slices imitation bacon, cooked crisp and crumbled, for the bacon.

Moussaka Stuffed Spud

2 baked potatoes
1 tablespoon extra-virgin olive oil
1 small onion, finely chopped
1 garlic clove, finely chopped
2 tablespoons finely chopped parsley
½ cup tomato sauce
¼ cup dry red wine
⅛ teaspoon ground mace
½ teaspoon oregano, crushed in a mortar with a pestle
½ cup white sauce (see Index)
½ cup finely chopped cooked lamb
½ cup grated 20% fat-reduced Monterey Jack cheese
¼ cup freshly grated Parmesan cheese

1. Cut a thin slice from the top of each potato. Remove the pulp from the potatoes, being careful not to tear the shells. Place the potato pulp in a mixing bowl and mash; cover and set aside. Keep the shells warm.

2. Heat the oil in a skillet. Add the onion and garlic and cook over low heat until tender, about 10 minutes. Add the parsley, tomato sauce, wine, mace, and oregano. Mix well and simmer for 30 minutes, stirring occasionally.

3. Remove from the heat. Add the mashed potato, white sauce, lamb, and half of both cheeses; mix well. Heat thoroughly.

4. Heap the mixture into the warm potato shells and top each potato with 2 tablespoons grated Monterey Jack cheese and 1 tablespoon grated Parmesan cheese. Heat in a 350°F oven until the cheese has melted.

Makes two servings.
Each serving contains approximately 613 calories, 89 mg cholesterol, 28 gm fat, 932 mg sodium.

Variation: VEGETARIAN GREEK STUFFED SPUD. Omit the lamb.

Mem Sahib's Chutney Potato

"Mem Sahib" was the term used for British wives in India; this recipe is an adaptation of one of their favorite India-inspired dishes.

2 tablespoons chopped walnuts
2 baked potatoes
2 teaspoons canola oil
½ cup chopped green onions, including the tops
½ cup plain nonfat yogurt
1 teaspoon curry powder
¼ cup chopped chutney
¾ cup cubed cooked lamb
Chopped egg white, raisins, pineapple, or any other classic
    condiments (optional)

1. Toast the walnuts in a 350°F oven for 8 to 10 minutes, or until golden brown. Watch them carefully as they burn easily. Set aside.

2. Cut the potatoes into halves. Scoop out the potato pulp, being careful not to tear the shells. Mash the pulp well and set aside in a covered bowl. Keep the potato shells warm.

3. Heat the oil in a skillet. Add the chopped green onions and cook over low heat until tender, about 10 minutes.

4. Combine the yogurt, curry powder, chutney, mashed potatoes, lamb, and walnuts, and add to the cooked onion in the skillet. Mix well and heat to serving temperature.

5. Heap the mixture into the warm potato shells. Serve with an assortment of classic condiments if desired.

Makes two servings.
Each serving contains approximately 521 calories, 86 mg cholesterol, 16 gm fat, 211 mg sodium.

Hot Dog and Sauerkraut Spud

2 baked potatoes
2 tablespoons corn-oil margarine
1 cup sauerkraut, undrained
2 chicken or turkey franks (hot dogs), chopped into small cubes
1 tablespoon prepared brown mustard
Chopped parsley, for garnish

1. Cut a thin slice from the top of each potato. Remove the pulp from the potatoes, being careful not to tear the shells. Place the potato pulp in a mixing bowl. Keep the shells warm.

2. Add the margarine to the potatoes and mash. Add the undrained sauerkraut, chopped hot dogs, and mustard, and stir until the mixture is thoroughly mixed.

3. Heap the mixture into the warm potato shells. Bake in a 350°F oven for 10 to 15 minutes, or until the desired serving temperature is reached. Sprinkle with parsley.

Makes two servings.
Each serving contains approximately 407 calories, 48 mg cholesterol, 20 gm fat, 1681 mg sodium.

Variation: Add ½ teaspoon caraway seeds to the potato mixture.

Sausage and Corn Spud

2 baked potatoes
¼ cup nonfat milk
⅓ cup light sour cream
1 teaspoon corn-oil margarine
¾ cup chopped smoked turkey sausage
1 cup cooked whole-kernel corn
1 teaspoon chopped parsley
¼ teaspoon salt
⅛ teaspoon freshly ground black pepper
Seasoned bread crumbs, for garnish
Chopped parsley, for garnish (optional)

1. Cut a thin slice from the top of each potato. Remove the pulp from the potatoes, being careful not to tear the shells. Place the potato pulp in a saucepan and mash. Keep the shells warm.

2. Add the milk, sour cream, margarine, and sausage to the mashed potato and mix thoroughly. Cook over low heat for 5 minutes. Add the corn, parsley, salt, and pepper, and continue to cook, stirring lightly, until the mixture is thoroughly heated.

3. Heap the mixture into the warm potato shells and garnish with seasoned bread crumbs or chopped parsley.

Makes two servings.
Each serving contains approximately 470 calories, 64 mg cholesterol, 17 gm fat, 955 mg sodium.

113

Stadium Tailgate Party Spud

Pack them in a thermal chest to take with you out to the ball game; if you don't have the chest, they're also good cold.

2 baked potatoes
1 tablespoon canola oil
½ cup chopped onion
2 chicken or turkey franks (hot dogs), chopped
2 tablespoons prepared mustard
2 tablespoons sweet pickle relish
⅛ teaspoon freshly ground black pepper
¾ cup white sauce (see Index)
Snipped chives or green onion tops, for garnish

1. Cut a thin slice from the top of each potato. Remove the pulp from the potatoes, being careful not to tear the shells. Place the potato pulp in a mixing bowl and mash; cover and set aside. Keep the shells warm.

2. Heat the oil in a large skillet. Add the onion and cook over low heat until tender, about 10 minutes. Add the chopped hot dogs and cook until heated through.

3. Combine the mustard, relish, and pepper and set aside. Heat the white sauce; add the mashed potatoes and mix well. Add the mustard and relish mixture to the potato mixture and mix well. Add to the onion and hot dogs and mix well.

4. Heap the mixture into the warm potato shells and garnish with snipped chives or green onion tops.

Makes two servings.
Each serving contains approximately 514 calories, 55 mg cholesterol, 26 gm fat, 1293 mg sodium.

Variation: STADIUM TAILGATE PARTY SPUD WITH CHEESE. Sprinkle 2 tablespoons grated 20% fat-reduced cheddar cheese on top of each potato. Place under the broiler until the cheese has melted.

FRUIT & VEGETABLE STUFFED SPUDS

Fruit and vegetable stuffed spuds offer exciting combinations of tastes and textures. The addition of nuts and seeds in some of these recipes adds still more variety in texture.

These recipes are all perfect for even strict vegetarian diets. They also run the gamut in menu planning from great breakfast ideas such as Pina Colada Spud (which is even good for dessert) to wonderfully different dinners like Chili Bowl Spuds or Lentil Stuffed Spuds. I also couldn't resist doing a dessert-in-a-spud, the delightfully different Potato and Raisin "Pudding" Spud. If you love raisin-rice pudding as much as I do, you'll love this variation!

The Simple Soup Spud is indeed simple – quick, easy, and inexpensive. For a more gourmet approach to soup in a spud, try the Vichyssoise in a Spud.

Creamed Vegetarian Stuffed Spud

¼ cup chopped raw almonds
2 baked potatoes
1 tablespoon corn-oil margarine
¼ cup chopped onion
¼ cup chopped green bell pepper
¾ cup cooked tempeh
3 tablespoons dry white wine
2 tablespoons chopped pimiento
2 tablespoons chopped parsley
¼ teaspoon salt
¼ teaspoon freshly ground black pepper
1 cup white sauce (see Index)
¼ cup nonfat milk
Pinch of paprika
Pimiento strips, for garnish (optional)

1. Toast the almonds in a 350°F oven for 8 to 10 minutes, or until golden brown. Watch them carefully as they burn easily. Set aside.

2. Cut a thin slice from the top of each potato. Remove the pulp from the potatoes, being careful not to tear the shells. Place the potato pulp in a mixing bowl and mash; cover and set aside. Keep the shells warm.

3. Heat the margarine in a large skillet. Add the onion and bell pepper and cook over low heat until tender, about 10 minutes. Add the tempeh, wine, pimiento, parsley, salt, and pepper, and mix well. Stir in the white sauce.

4. Add the milk to the mashed potato mixture; mix well. Add to the ingredients in the skillet and cook to serving temperature. Add the toasted almonds within the last minute of cooking.

5. Heap the mixture into the warm potato shells, sprinkle with paprika, and garnish with pimiento strips.

Makes two servings.
Each serving contains approximately 705 calories, 1 mg cholesterol, 35 gm fat, 757 mg sodium.

Chili Bowl Spud

2 baked potatoes
1 tablespoon canola oil
1 small onion, finely chopped
1 garlic clove, finely chopped
1 teaspoon chili powder
¼ teaspoon ground cumin seed
⅛ teaspoon oregano, crushed in a mortar with a pestle
¼ teaspoon salt
Pinch of freshly ground black pepper
1 large tomato, peeled and diced
½ cup cooked kidney beans
4 tablespoons grated 20% fat-reduced cheddar cheese (optional)

1. Cut a thin slice from the top of each potato. Remove the pulp from the potatoes, being careful not to tear the shells. Place the potato pulp in a mixing bowl and mash; cover and set aside. Keep the shells warm.

2. Heat the oil in a skillet. Add the onion and garlic, and cook over low heat until soft, about 10 minutes. Add the chili powder, cumin seed, oregano, salt, and pepper. Mix well. Add the diced tomato and mashed potato; simmer for 15 minutes. Add the cooked beans and mix well.

3. Heap the chili into the potato "bowls" and top with grated cheese if desired. Heat in a 350°F oven for 10 minutes, or until the cheese has melted.

Makes two servings.
Each serving contains approximately 389 calories, 12 mg cholesterol, 11 gm fat, 373 mg sodium.

Lentil Stuffed Spud

2 baked potatoes
2 tablespoons canola oil
¼ cup chopped onion
1 garlic clove, minced or pressed
¼ cup grated scraped carrot
2 cups canned tomatoes, drained and chopped
¼ cup chopped green bell pepper
¼ teaspoon salt
¼ teaspoon freshly ground black pepper
½ teaspoon marjoram, crushed in a mortar with a pestle
1 cup cooked lentils
Chopped parsley, snipped chives, or green onion tops, for garnish

1. Cut a thin slice from the top of each potato. Remove the pulp from the potatoes, being careful not to tear the shells. Place the potato pulp in a mixing bowl and mash; cover and set aside.

2. Heat the oil in a skillet. Add the onion and garlic, and cook over low heat until tender, about 10 minutes. Add the carrot, tomatoes, bell pepper, salt, pepper, and marjoram, and mix thoroughly. Add the lentils and potato and combine well.

3. Heap the mixture into the potato shells and place them in a baking dish. Cover, and bake at 375°F for 1 hour. Garnish with chopped parsley, chives, or green onion tops.

Makes two servings.
Each serving contains approximately 480 calories, no cholesterol, 15 gm fat, 710 mg sodium.

Variation: LENTIL STUFFED SPUD AU GRATIN. Sprinkle 2 tablespoons grated Monterey Jack or cheddar cheese over the top of each potato. Place under the broiler until the cheese has melted.

Masala Dosa Stuffed Spud

(Indian Sandwich)

The Masala Dosa Stuffed Spud is delicious served with sliced tomatoes. Add fresh fruit for dessert and you have a filling and unusual vegetarian meal.

2 baked potatoes
1 tablespoon canola oil
1 small onion, finely chopped
1 garlic clove, minced or pressed
2 canned green chiles, drained, seeded and finely chopped
¼ teaspoon ground turmeric
¼ teaspoon ground ginger
½ teaspoon chili powder
½ teaspoon ground coriander
½ teaspoon ground cumin seed
¼ teaspoon salt
¼ cup nonfat milk
2 tablespoons finely chopped parsley

1. Cut the baked potatoes into halves. Remove the pulp from the potatoes, being careful not to tear the shells. Place potato pulp in a mixing bowl and mash; cover and set aside. Keep the shells warm.

2. Heat the oil in a skillet. Add the onion, garlic, and chiles and cook over low heat until tender, about 10 minutes. Add all of the spices, the salt, and milk, mix well and heat through.

3. Divide the mixture evenly into the 4 potato shells. Eat like open-faced sandwiches.

Makes two servings.
Each serving contains approximately 284 calories, 1 mg cholesterol, 8 gm fat, 333 mg sodium.

Stuffed Spud Stroganoff

This is a wonderful entree for a Russian vegetarian dinner.

2 baked potatoes
1 tablespoon corn-oil margarine
1 small onion, thinly sliced
¼ pound fresh mushrooms, sliced (1 cup)
½ teaspoon paprika
½ teaspoon basil, crushed in a mortar with a pestle
⅛ teaspoon freshly grated nutmeg
¼ teaspoon salt
¼ teaspoon freshly ground black pepper
2 tablespoons sherry
½ cup light sour cream
Chopped parsley, for garnish (optional)

1. Cut a thin slice from the top of each potato. Remove the pulp from the potatoes, being careful not to tear the shells. Place the potato pulp in a mixing bowl and mash; cover and set aside. Keep the shells warm.

2. Heat the margarine in a skillet. Add the onion and mushrooms, and cook over low heat until tender, about 10 minutes. Add the paprika, basil, nutmeg, salt, pepper, sherry, and mashed potato and cook for 5 minutes. Add the sour cream and mix thoroughly. Heat through.

3. Heap the mixture into the warm potato shells and serve at once. Garnish with chopped parsley if desired.

Makes two servings.
Each serving contains approximately 353 calories, 23 mg cholesterol, 14 gm fat, 402 mg sodium.

Variations: STUFFED SPUD BEEF, CHICKEN, OR TURKEY STROGANOFF. Add ¾ cup chopped cooked lean beef, chicken, or turkey in step 3.

Guacamole Stuffed Spud

The Guacamole Stuffed Spud is another delightful surprise. Not only is it delicious and certainly different, but it considerably reduces the calories per spoonful of guacamole because potatoes are so much lower in calories than avocados.

2 baked potatoes
1 large ripe avocado, peeled and seeded
1 tablespoon freshly squeezed lemon juice
2 tablespoons finely chopped onion
¾ teaspoon salt
¼ teaspoon ground cumin seed
¼ teaspoon chili powder
¼ teaspoon garlic powder
1 tablespoon light sour cream
1 large tomato, diced
Dash of Tabasco
Chopped green onions, for garnish

1. Cut a thin slice from the top of each potato. Remove the pulp from the potatoes, being careful not to tear the shells. Place the potato pulp in a mixing bowl and mash; cover and chill.

2. Mash the avocado until there are no lumps. Add the lemon juice, onion, salt, cumin, chili powder, garlic powder, and sour cream; mix well.

3. Add avocado mixture to the mashed potatoes and mix thoroughly. Fold in the diced tomato and Tabasco and stir lightly until thoroughly mixed.

4. Heap the mixture into the potato shells and garnish with chopped green onions.

Makes two servings.
Each serving contains approximately 425 calories, 3 mg cholesterol, 24 gm fat, 922 mg sodium.

Pritikin Stuffed Spud

This recipe was developed for an afternoon snack at the Pritikin Longevity Center in Santa Monica.

2 baked potatoes
2 tablespoons hoop cheese, crumbled
½ cup buttermilk
1 tablespoon chopped fresh parsley
2 teaspoons low sodium Dijon-style mustard
Pinch dill weed

1. Slit (do not halve) the baked potatoes and carefully remove the pulp into a bowl. Keep the shells warm for refilling.

2. Add all other ingredients to the potato pulp and mix with an electric mixer until well blended.

3. Refill the potato shells with the mixture. Place on a baking sheet and bake at 350°F for 30 minutes.

Makes two servings.
Each serving contains approximately 211 calories, 3 mg cholesterol, 1 gm fat, 146 mg sodium.

Vichyssoise in a Spud

Serving vichyssoise in a spud bowl is an imaginative presentation for an informal patio supper, and it goes well with charcoal-broiled fish, meat, or poultry.

2 baked potatoes
3 tablespoons chopped onion
¼ cup chicken stock (see Index)
2 tablespoons nonfat milk
2 tablespoons light sour cream
Pinch of salt (omit if using salted stock)
Pinch of freshly ground black pepper
¼ teaspoon freshly squeezed lemon juice
Chopped chives, for garnish

1. Cut a thin slice from the top of each potato. Remove the pulp, being careful not to tear the shells. Dice the potato pulp and set aside. Place the shells, covered, in the refrigerator.

2. Combine chopped onion and chicken stock in a saucepan and bring to a boil. Add the potato pulp, reduce heat, and simmer covered for 10 minutes.

3. Spoon mixture into a blender container or food processor, add all other ingredients except chopped chives and potato shells, and blend until smooth. Cover and refrigerate until cold. When cold, pour the soup into each potato "bowl" and garnish with chopped chives.

Makes two servings.
Each serving contains approximately 265 calories, 4 mg cholesterol, 2 gm fat, 120 mg sodium.

Borscht Spud

2 baked potatoes
½ cup light sour cream
1 (8-ounce) can beets, drained
1 teaspoon freshly squeezed lemon juice
⅛ teaspoon onion salt
⅛ teaspoon freshly ground black pepper
Light sour cream, for garnish

1. Cut a thin slice from the top of each potato. Remove the pulp from the potatoes, being careful not to tear the shells. Place the potato pulp in a mixing bowl and mash; cover and set aside. Set the shells aside.

2. Combine the sour cream, drained beets, lemon juice, onion salt, and pepper in a blender container. Cover and blend until smooth.

3. Pour the puréed beet mixture into the mashed potatoes and mix thoroughly. Spoon into the potato shells and garnish with a dollop of sour cream. Good served hot or cold.

Makes two servings.
Each serving contains approximately 283 calories, 23 mg cholesterol, 8 gm fat, 357 mg sodium.

Simple Soup Spud

2 baked potatoes
½ cup heated leftover soup (any kind)

1. Cut a thin slice from the top of each potato. Remove the pulp from the potatoes, being careful not to tear the shells. Place the potato pulp in a mixing bowl.

2. Add the heated leftover soup to the potato pulp and mix lightly. Spoon mixture into the potato shells. Good hot or cold.

Makes two servings.
Nutritional information will vary depending upon the soup used.

Get-Well Chicken Soup in a Spud

1 baked potato
¼ cup heated chicken stock (see Index)

1. Cut a thin slice from the top of the potato. Using a spoon, break up the pulp in the potato. Pour the hot chicken stock evenly over the potato.

2. Serve to the patient immediately!

Makes one serving containing approximately 160 calories, no cholesterol, negligible fat, 14 mg sodium.

Peanut Butter and Jelly Spud

This is a fine after-school snack for hungry students. The potatoes are also a delicious and unusual breakfast. Serve hot or cold, depending upon the weather!

2 baked potatoes
¼ cup nonfat milk
½ cup unhomogenized peanut butter
¼ cup grape jelly (or your favorite kind)

1. Cut a thin slice from the top of each potato. Remove the pulp from the potatoes, being careful not to tear the shells. Place the potato pulp and milk in a mixing bowl and whip until smooth. Set the shells aside.

2. Fold the peanut butter and jelly into the potato mixture, leaving streaks of peanut butter and jelly through the mixture. Heap into the potato shells and garnish each with a dollop of jelly.

Makes two servings.
Each serving contains approximately 611 calories, 1 mg cholesterol, 32 gm fat, 81 mg sodium.

Banana and Peanut Butter Snack Spud

2 baked potatoes
½ cup unhomogenized peanut butter
2 small bananas, mashed
¼ cup nonfat milk
¼ teaspoon freshly grated nutmeg or ground cinnamon
Nutmeg, for garnish

1. Cut the baked potatoes into halves. Remove the pulp from the potatoes, being careful not to tear the shells. Place the potato pulp in a mixing bowl and mash.

2. Combine the peanut butter, mashed bananas, milk, and spice and add to the mashed potato. Mix with an electric mixer until very smooth.

3. Spoon the mixture into the potato shells and refrigerate for after-school snacks. Sprinkle with a little nutmeg before serving.

Makes four snack-size servings.
Each serving contains approximately 321 calories, negligible cholesterol, 16 gm fat, 18 mg sodium.

128

Vegetarian Spud

2 baked potatoes
½ cup sliced mushrooms
2 tablespoons corn-oil margarine
¼ teaspoon ground ginger
⅛ teaspoon freshly grated nutmeg
¼ teaspoon salt
⅛ teaspoon freshly ground black pepper
1 cup assorted chopped leftover cooked vegetables
¼ cup diced raw apple
½ cup light sour cream
Chopped parsley, for garnish

1. Cut a thin slice from the top of each potato. Remove the pulp from the potatoes, being careful not to tear the shells. Place the potato pulp in a mixing bowl and mash; cover and set aside. Keep the shells warm.

2. Heat the margarine in a saucepan. Sauté the sliced mushrooms over low heat for about 5 minutes, stirring frequently. Add the ginger, nutmeg, salt, and pepper and mix well. Add the vegetables and the raw apple; stir well.

3. Add the sour cream to the mashed potatoes and mix thoroughly. Add the vegetable mixture and continue to heat, stirring constantly, until thoroughly heated. Heap the mixture into the warm potato shells. Garnish with chopped parsley.

Makes two servings.
Each serving contains approximately 390 calories, 23 mg cholesterol, 19 gm fat, 470 mg sodium.

Potato and Raisin "Pudding" Spud

2 baked potatoes
2 tablespoons nonfat milk
2 tablespoons sugar
Pinch of salt
1 teaspoon ground cinnamon
1½ teaspoons vanilla extract
3 tablespoons raisins

1. Cut a thin slice from the top of each potato. Remove the pulp, being careful not to tear the shells. Dice the potato pulp and set the shells aside.

2. Put the potato pulp in a food processor with a metal blade. Add all other ingredients except the raisins and blend until satin smooth. Transfer the mixture to a bowl, add the raisins, and mix well.

3. Spoon the "pudding" into a number 7 pastry tube with a tip which is large enough for raisins to be piped through and pipe the "pudding" back into the potato shells. Bake in a 350°F oven for 20 minutes.

Makes two servings.

Each serving contains approximately 130 calories, negligible cholesterol, negligible fat, 108 mg sodium.

Pina Colada Spud

This recipe was inspired by the famous tropical drink and is just as habit-forming! The Pina Colada Spud is excellent as a light luncheon entree served with cold poached fish or chicken. It also makes an unusual and nutritious dessert.

1 (8-ounce) can pineapple chunks, packed in natural juice
2 baked potatoes
½ cup low-fat milk
2 teaspoons pineapple juice (reserved from the can of pineapple)
1½ teaspoons vanilla extract
1 teaspoon coconut extract
1 tablespoon fructose
Cinnamon, for garnish

1. Drain the juice from the can of pineapple, reserving 2 teaspoons for use in the recipe (the rest is a delicious cold beverage). Set the pineapple aside.

2. Cut the potatoes into halves. Allow to cool to room temperature. Remove the pulp from the potato halves carefully. Place the pulp in a bowl and mash.

3. Add the milk and reserved pineapple juice to the mashed potatoes and mix well until a smooth consistency is attained. Add the vanilla, coconut extract, and fructose to the potato mixture. Fold in the pineapple chunks.

4. Heap the mixture into the potato halves and garnish with cinnamon.

Makes two servings.
Each serving contains approximately 312 calories, 5 mg cholesterol, 1 gm fat, 41 mg sodium.

Mincemeat Stuffed Spud

This unusual stuffed spud is delicious served with a fresh fruit and cottage cheese salad in place of a sweet roll or Danish pastry, During the holidays serve this spud with sliced turkey and scrambled eggs for brunch. Garnish the plate with a few cranberries for color.

2 baked potatoes
2 tablespoons corn-oil margarine
½ cup low-fat milk
1 (9-ounce) box condensed mincemeat
Ground cinnamon, for garnish
Cinnamon sticks, for garnish (optional)

1. Cut the potatoes into halves. Remove the pulp from the potatoes, being careful not to tear the shells. Add the margarine to the potato pulp and mash. Set the shells aside.

2. Add the milk, a little at a time, to the potatoes, mashing to a creamy consistency. Crumble the mincemeat and add it to the potato mixture. Mix thoroughly.

3. Heap filling into the potato shells. Sprinkle lightly with ground cinnamon and garnish with pieces of cinnamon sticks, if desired.

Makes two servings.
Each serving contains approximately 745 calories, 5 mg cholesterol, 17 gm fat, 796 mg sodium.

INDEX

Alpenspitz Stuffed Spud with
  Mushroom Sauce, 105
Avocado, 121

Bacon Quiche Spud, 99
Baked potato, 14
Baked Tuna in a Spud, 63
Banana Breakfast Spud, 30
Banana and Peanut Butter Snack
  Spud, 128
Bean Burrito Spud, 40
Beef Hash in a Spud, 86
Beef Quiche Spud, 99
Beef stock, 18
Beer & Pretzel Spud, 35
BLT Stuffed Spud, 109
Borscht Spud, 124
Bouillabaisse Stuffed Spud, 48

Calories, 10
Canyon Ranch Stuft Spud, 32
Cheese, 25
Chicken Casserole Spud, 66
Chicken and Cheese Stuffed Spud, 75
Chicken Florentine Stuffed Spud, 76
Chicken Hash in a Spud, 81
Chicken stock, 17
Chicken Surprise Stuffed Spud, 74

Chicken Tarragon Stuffed Spud, 73
Chicken with Dill Sauce in a Spud, 46
Chicken Véronique Stuffed Spud, 47
Chili Bowl Spud, 117
Chopped Chicken Livers in a Spud, 77
Chopstick Tuna Spud, 64
Chutney and Chicken Spud, 71
Classic Caviar Spud, 49
Corned Beef and Cabbage Spud, 90
Crab & Swiss Cheese Spud, 50
Creamed Chicken Stuffed Spud, 72
Creamed Tuna Stuffed Spud, 65
Creamed Vegetarian Stuffed Spud, 116
Cumin Dressing, 23
Curried Chicken in Spuds, 70
Curried Crab in Spuds, 51
Curry Dressing, 23

Deviled Ham Stuffed Spud, 104
Dilled Fish Stuffed Spud Amandine, 46
Dried Beef in a Spud, 94

Eclectic Salad in Potato Pockets, 83
Eggs, 25
Egg Foo Yung Spud, 26
Enchiladas de Papas, 39

Famine, 9-10

Fiber, 10
Fish, 45
Fish Florentine Stuffed Spud, 76
Fish stock, 19
Fish Véronique Stuffed Spud, 47
Freezing, 12
Fructose, 24
Fruit, 115

German Pork and Cabbage Spud, 97
Get-Well Chicken Soup in a Spud, 126
Gravlax, 60
Gravlax Stuffed Spud, 59
Green Eggs and Ham in Spuds, 100
Guacamole Stuffed Spud, 121

Ham Quiche Spud, 99
Ham Soufflé in Spuds, 103
Ham Surprise Stuffed Spud, 74
History, 9
Hollandaise sauce, 21
Hot Dog and Sauerkraut Spud, 112
Hot German Potato Salad, 108

Indian Sandwich Stuffed Spud, 119
Irish Lamb Stew Stuffed Spud, 98
Irish Taco, 93
Italian Dressing, 23

Jansson's Temptation in a Spud, 68
Jet Fuel dressing, 23

Lentil Stuffed Spud, 118
Lentil Stuffed Spud au Gratin, 118
Lined potato bowls, 16
Liver and Onion Stuffed Spud, 96
Lox 'n' Spuds, 61

Masala Dosa Stuffed Spud, 119
Meat, 85
Mem Sahib's Chutney Potato, 111
Mincemeat Stuffed Spud, 132
Moussaka Stuffed Spud, 110

New England Stuffed Spud, 87

Northern Italian Stuffed Spud, 43

Overbaked Potato, 15
Oyster Stew Spuds, 54

Papas Refritos con Queso, 40
Pâté in a Spud, 77
Peanut Butter and Jelly Spud, 127
Peas and Ham Spud, 102
Pina Colada Spud, 131
Pizza Potato, 41
Pizza Sauce, 22
Potato-Cheese Soufflé in Spuds, 28
Potato Chicken Relleno, 42
Potato Enchiladas, 39
Potato Lasagna, 92
Potato & Onion au Gratin, 37
Potato Primavera Spud, 33
Potato and Raisin "Pudding" Spud, 130
Potato Relleno, 42
Poultry, 69
Pritikin Stuffed Spud, 122

Rarebit in a Spud, 36
Refried Potatoes with Cheese, 40
Reuben Spud, 89
Runner's Stuffed Spud, 31

Salade Niçoise Spud, 67
Sausage and Corn Spud, 113
Sauces, 20-22, 24
Seafood, 45
Seafood Curry with Capers Spud, 57
Seafood Stew Spud, 58
Shrimp Salad in a Spud, 53
Simple Soup Spud, 125
Skins, 11
Sloppy Joe Spud, 88
Sockeye Salmon Spud, 62
Southern Turnip Stuffed Spud, 107
Speedy Clam Spud, 56
Spicy Clam Stuffed Spud, 55
Spuds Benedict, 106
Spud "Crepes" Florentine, 38
Spud Oscar, 52

Stadium Tailgate Party Spud, 114
  with Cheese, 114
Steak Tartare Stuffed Spud, 95
Stock, 17-19, 24
Stuffed Spud Marco Polo, 78
Stuffed Spud Stroganoff, 120
  with Beef, Chicken or Turkey, 120

Tarragon Dressing, 23
Tex-Mex Chili Spud, 91
Tofu Stuffed Spud, 29
Tuna Casserole Spud, 66
Turkey and Cranberry Spud, 79
Turkey Hash in a Spud, 81

Turkey Vegetable Spud, 80

Vegetables, 115
Vegetable Stuffed Spud, 34
Vegetarian BLT Stuffed Spud, 109
Vegetarian "Chicken" Relleno, 42
Vegetarian "Chicken" with Dill Sauce in a
  Spud, 46
Vegetarian Greek Stuffed Spud, 110
Vegetarian Quiche Spud, 27
Vegetarian Spud, 129
Vichyssoise in a Spud, 123
White Chili Bowl Spud, 82
White sauce, 20